DAEMONIUM MARIS

The Leviathan Doctrine

Seth Helix

CONTENTS

Title Page
INTRODUCTION: BENEATH THE WATERS, A SERPENT WAITS — 1
CHAPTER ONE: ORIGINS IN CHAOS – LEVIATHAN IN ANCIENT MYTH — 4
CHAPTER TWO: LEVIATHAN IN THE SHADOWS OF SCRIPTURE AND LORE — 7
CHAPTER THREE: FROM MONSTER TO MONARCH — 10
CHAPTER FOUR: LEVIATHAN IN MODERN OCCULTISM AND SATANIC TRADITION — 14
CHAPTER FIVE: WHISPERS BENEATH THE SURFACE — 19
CHAPTER SIX: THE MIRROR AS ABYSS — 23
CHAPTER SEVEN: POSSESSION AND MERGING WHEN LEVIATHAN ENTERS — 28
CHAPTER EIGHT: LEVIATHAN THE PRIMEVAL FORCE — 33
CHAPTER NINE: THE SUMMONING OF LEVIATHAN — 38
CHAPTER TEN: LEVIATHANIC MAGICK THE CURRENTS BENEATH — 43
CHAPTER ELEVEN: LEVIATHAN AND LEGION THE MOUTH OF MANY — 47
CHAPTER TWELVE: RITUALS TO EVOKE LEVIATHAN — 52
CHAPTER THIRTEEN: LEVIATHANS ROLE IN THE DARK FEMININE AND SHADOW MASCULINE — 58

CHAPTER FOURTEEN: LEVIATHAN IN THE OCCULT THE ABYSSAL FORCE IN ESOTERIC TRADITION	64
CHAPTER FIFTEEN: RITUALS AND CORRESPONDENCES	70
CHAPTER SIXTEEN: CHANTS AND HIDDEN KNOWLEDGE	76
Chapter Seventeen – Leviathan's Symbolic Web: Connections to Mythic Creatures and Occult Archetypes	81
CHAPTER EIGHTEEN: SHADOWS IN INK SECRET SCROLLS AND FORBIDDEN TEXTS ON LEVIATHAN	87
CHAPTER NINETEEN: RITUAL WORK WITH LEVIATHAN	93
CHAPTER TWENTY: FINAL WORDS THE SERPENT BENEATH ALL THINGS	99
ABOUT THE AUTHOR	103

INTRODUCTION: BENEATH THE WATERS, A SERPENT WAITS

In the oldest myths of mankind, water has always been a symbol of the unknown—vast, untamable, and filled with danger. The sea, in its immense and shadowed depths, has stirred both awe and terror since the dawn of civilization. From this murky womb of mystery emerged a name feared across time and cultures: Leviathan.

The name alone conjures images of a colossal serpent, an ancient beast coiled in the darkest trenches of the ocean, waiting to rise. But Leviathan is not merely a monster of the deep—it is an idea, a force, and perhaps, a presence that still lingers in the margins of reality. More than any other creature from the biblical and occult world, Leviathan has evolved into a symbol of chaos, pride, envy, and rebellion. A demon of deep emotion and darker intellect. A gatekeeper to realms we were never meant to touch.

In the pages of the Hebrew Bible, Leviathan is described as a terrifying sea monster, created by God as a demonstration of divine power. In Job, Psalms, and Isaiah, it is depicted as untamable, invulnerable, and destined for destruction at the hands of the Creator in the end times. To the Israelites, it represented the chaos that God had subdued at the beginning of creation—a lingering threat from a primordial past.

But as time passed and belief systems transformed, so too did Leviathan. With the rise of Christianity and its need to catalogue the infernal, Leviathan became not just a monster, but a demon—a grand adversary in the unfolding cosmic battle between good and evil. Medieval demonologists placed Leviathan among the highest of infernal beings, ranking him as one of the Seven Princes of Hell and assigning him dominion over the deadly sin of envy. In this role, Leviathan becomes not only a creature of watery ruin but of emotional corrosion—the whisperer of jealousy, the stirrer of rage, the divider of hearts.

This is the duality of Leviathan: both beast and spirit, physical and abstract, a terror of the oceans and a corruptor of the soul.

To occultists and esoteric practitioners, Leviathan has taken on additional layers of meaning. In ceremonial magic, the demon is sometimes invoked in complex rituals involving the water element, astral travel, or the unlocking of forbidden knowledge. In Satanic traditions, Leviathan is often associated with the western cardinal point, the subconscious mind, and the serpentine pathways between realms. To summon Leviathan is to gaze into the abyss of oneself—into desire, envy, emotion, and transformation. Some warn it is a gate that cannot be closed once opened.

Yet even now, Leviathan is not confined to dusty grimoires and crumbling scriptures. The demon continues to appear in art, literature, dreams, and even alleged modern encounters. Those who report visions of Leviathan describe immense shapes seen beneath the surface of oceans and lakes, voices from the water calling to them in sleep, or a sensation of being watched by something unfathomably ancient. These accounts often share a common theme: the overwhelming presence of envy, rage, or inner disquiet that accompanies such sightings. Is this collective symbolism? Or something more?

This book seeks to uncover the many faces of Leviathan—historical, spiritual, occult, and experiential. We will begin with the mythic sea dragons of Babylon and Ugarit, where chaos monsters first slithered across creation stories. We will trace the evolution of Leviathan through Judaic and Christian texts, into the hellish catalogues of demonologists. We will examine its place in esoteric orders and magical traditions, and analyze its psychological interpretations in modern occultism and shadow work.

And we will listen to the whispers—those firsthand accounts from individuals who claim to have felt the presence of Leviathan in waking life. Whether hallucination or revelation, these testimonies raise a chilling question: What if Leviathan is not just a story? What if it waits?

To understand Leviathan is to stare into what lies beneath the surface—not only of the world, but of the self. Leviathan embodies the chaos we fear, the emotions we suppress, and the envy that erodes. It is a mirror held up to our darkest reflections.

So dive with caution.

Once you gaze into the abyss, Leviathan might gaze back.

CHAPTER ONE: ORIGINS IN CHAOS – LEVIATHAN IN ANCIENT MYTH

Before Leviathan was ever named a demon, long before it was catalogued in grimoires or feared by Christian mystics, it existed in the murky waters of myth as something far more ancient and primal. Leviathan's true story begins not in Hell, but in the abyssal depths of pre-biblical imagination, where sea serpents and chaos dragons ruled the narratives of the earliest civilizations. To understand Leviathan is to trace the serpent's lineage back to the dawn of belief itself, when humanity first gazed at the ocean and saw in its endless blackness a reflection of fear, mystery, and divine conflict.

The myth of a monstrous sea serpent appears in some of the oldest written records of the human race. In ancient Mesopotamia, the Babylonians spoke of Tiamat, the saltwater goddess of primordial chaos. Tiamat was not a demon in the modern sense, but a creator and destroyer in one. She gave birth to the first gods but later turned against them, rising up in a cataclysmic battle. In the Babylonian creation epic, the Enuma Elish, the storm god Marduk confronts her in her terrible dragon form. He defeats her and slices her vast body in two—using one half to form the sky, the other to form the earth. Tiamat was the sea, the storm, the unknown void, and the violent, swirling chaos before the order of the world. In many ways, she was Leviathan's grandmother, a mythic blueprint upon which later civilizations would build their own stories of cosmic rebellion and divine dominion.

From this mythic origin point, the idea of a monstrous sea serpent spread across the cultures of the Near East. In the coastal kingdom of Ugarit, a city that thrived in what is now Syria, a strikingly similar legend took shape. Their storm god, Baal Hadad, fought a creature named Lotan, a multi-headed serpent described as the "twisting" or "fleeing" serpent of the sea. This was no ordinary serpent. It was a seven-headed beast, a direct symbolic representation of chaotic multiplicity and overwhelming disorder. In this mythology, Baal's victory over Lotan allowed for the stabilization of the world and the establishment of divine kingship. The echoes of this tale reverberate into the Old Testament and beyond.

When the early Hebrews developed their own spiritual narratives, they inherited not only cultural stories but also archetypes. In the Hebrew Bible, Leviathan makes its first terrifying appearance in the Book of Job, where it is described in poetic and thunderous detail. It is invincible, untamable, a creature of the deep feared by all but God Himself. Job 41 describes its scales as impenetrable, its breath as capable of igniting flames, and its heart as hard as stone. It is not merely a sea creature but a supernatural force, a living embodiment of divine power held in check only by the Creator.

In other parts of the Bible, such as Psalms and Isaiah, Leviathan is again mentioned as a being God has or will destroy. In Psalms 74:14, God crushes the heads of Leviathan and gives them as food to the creatures of the desert. In Isaiah 27:1, Leviathan is referred to as a "twisting serpent" and "the dragon that is in the sea," which God will slay at the end of days. This language mirrors the older Ugaritic texts describing Baal's battle with Lotan, suggesting that the biblical Leviathan is a direct spiritual successor—a mythic image passed from generation to generation, reshaped to fit monotheistic belief.

But Leviathan was not alone in Hebrew myth. Another sea monster, Rahab, appears in similar contexts. In Job and Isaiah, Rahab is also depicted as a force subdued by God. Scholars debate whether Rahab and Leviathan are the same being under different names or separate creatures representing different aspects of cosmic chaos. What is clear is that the Hebrews adopted and adapted this archetype of the chaos monster as a symbol of divine triumph. In these stories, God is not just a creator but a warrior who slays the forces of disorder.

Leviathan, then, serves a profound theological purpose. In a world where natural disasters, floods, and famine were seen as expressions of divine or demonic will, the sea became a potent symbol of danger and unpredictability. Leviathan embodied those fears—the threat that even after creation, chaos still lurked, waiting to rise again. The God of Israel, by subduing Leviathan, demonstrated ultimate authority over the very forces that had once threatened to undo the universe.

Yet Leviathan's tale did not end with these ancient victories. The creature lived on, transformed by later Jewish mystics and Christian demonologists into something far more personal and psychological. But even in these later interpretations, the ancient serpent of the deep retained its primordial terror. The fear of drowning, of being pulled into black depths, of facing something incomprehensible and vast—that fear still has a name. And that name is Leviathan.

In myth, Leviathan is not merely a monster; it is the memory of chaos itself. It is the tension between order and disorder, creation and destruction, God and the abyss. It is the thing that waits beneath, always just beneath, the surface.

And it never truly dies.

CHAPTER TWO: LEVIATHAN IN THE SHADOWS OF SCRIPTURE AND LORE

There is a creature that surfaces only briefly in sacred texts, but whose presence leaves a wake of dread. It is not described in full, nor is it clearly explained. Instead, it slithers between verses like a whisper — half-seen, half-understood. Leviathan.

In the ancient traditions of the Hebrews, Leviathan was more than legend. It was a living symbol of the chaos that once reigned before the world was set in order. A serpent of impossible size, armored in scales like iron, fire-breathing, and immune to any weapon forged by man. It was not a thing to be hunted or slain by human hands. It was a warning.

In the Book of Job, a grim figure of suffering and divine silence, Leviathan is given one of its most vivid portrayals. Here, the creature is not described with reverence — but with awe laced with terror. It cannot be subdued. Its body is a fortress. Fire spills from its jaws. Its heart is likened to stone, unfeeling and invincible. The description goes beyond natural horror — it's anatomical blasphemy. This is no animal. It is a primordial design from before the world was tamed.

Most importantly, it is said to be a king — not over land, but over all who are proud. This is a serpent that rules over the sins of man, not by force, but by reflection. Leviathan is not just beneath the sea — it is within the self.

In the oldest Jewish writings, Leviathan is said to have been one of two twin monsters — the other, a land creature known as Behemoth. Both were created before the formation of the world, both too dangerous to roam free. In the legends, the Leviathan is not destroyed, but hidden, locked beneath the waters. Chained, some say. Buried in the deep, others claim. Not dead. Never dead. Only sleeping. Watching.

According to some mystics, this creature is more than flesh — it is envy itself, jealousy incarnate. It coils not just in oceans, but in the souls of those who look upon others with hunger and hatred. In this form, Leviathan becomes a metaphysical infection, a spiritual poison that seeps into the heart of humanity. A parasite of the will.

There are darker stories, the ones not told from pulpits. In the scrolls of hidden rabbis and midnight scholars, Leviathan is seen as a gate — a living threshold between the surface world and the abyss. Those who dream of it too often are said to wake gasping, as if pulled from drowning. Some say the creature can speak — not with words, but with thoughts, buried and foul. It does not scream. It whispers. And what it whispers, you already believe.

The creature's association with water is no accident. Water is memory. Water is emotion. Water is the carrier of unseen things. In Leviathan's depths swim not only ancient fear, but the sins we refuse to surface. Leviathan is the weight pressing down on guilt, on rage, on grief too long drowned. It is the storm below the stillness.

Isaiah, one of the more cryptic voices in ancient lore, once spoke of Leviathan as a creature yet to be destroyed. Not in the past — but at the end. The implication is chilling. Leviathan has not yet been slain. It survives, waiting for the collapse of the world to rise once more. And when it does, it will not come alone.

Midrashic texts — ancient commentaries whispered among mystics — speak of Leviathan being devoured in a final feast at the end of days. But others say the opposite: that it is not the people who eat Leviathan, but Leviathan who devours the world. The ocean rising. The land swallowed. The fire of the deep unleashed at last.

In this duality lies the true terror: Leviathan is both myth and mirror. It is a beast, yes — a terror of scale and heat and depth. But more than that, it is what we bury. It is what we feed with every secret we keep, every bitterness we swallow, every jealous breath we pretend not to take. In Jewish lore, Leviathan is often treated with reluctant awe, not because of what it is — but because it is still there.

And worse: it may be us.

In the shadows of scripture, where fear was written in metaphor and symbols, Leviathan's name appears like a smudge of black ink — not erased, just smeared. Still present. Still watching.

The sea has not forgotten. And neither has the serpent.

CHAPTER THREE: FROM MONSTER TO MONARCH

The ocean, in ancient myth, was vast enough to house gods and monsters. But when Leviathan was pulled from the watery depths and cast into the black tomes of Christian theology, it was transformed into something even more insidious. It became not just a monster — but a demon. An immortal will. A fallen power. And perhaps, a king.

In the cold logic of medieval demonology, the chaotic was no longer sufficient. It had to be ordered. Catalogued. Bound in name, number, and sin. The early Church, obsessed with hierarchy, took the chaos-serpents of Hebrew tradition and hammered them into the iron frames of Hell's bureaucracy. Leviathan, coiled and patient, was fitted into a crown of corruption. It was not merely a memory of chaos now — it was a Prince of Envy, an entity commanding damnation itself.

Leviathan Among the Seven Princes of Hell

According to later demonologists such as Peter Binsfeld and Sebastien Michaelis, the Seven Deadly Sins were each ruled by a corresponding demon. Pride belonged to Lucifer. Wrath to Satan. Greed to Mammon. Lust to Asmodeus. Sloth to Belphegor. Gluttony to Beelzebub.

And envy — that slow-burning rot of the soul — belonged to

Leviathan.

This was no arbitrary assignment. Envy, unlike rage or pride, is subtle. It coils through the mind like a whisper, feeding discontent and poisoning relationships. It is the quiet malice behind a smile, the twisted joy at another's downfall. It is corrosive, slow, and intimate — just like Leviathan, whose very name in Hebrew implies coiling, writhing, and enclosure.

Leviathan, then, became more than a dragon. It became the embodiment of the jealous mind. Where Lucifer tempts through grandeur, Leviathan undermines through bitterness. It offers no kingdom, only the knowledge that someone else has one you do not.

This redefinition marked Leviathan's true horror. It was not an outside enemy, but an internal one. No longer only beneath the waves — but beneath the skin.

Infernal Forms and Shape-Shifting Doctrine

In occult grimoires and black books written in the shadows of monasteries and courts, Leviathan's form is ever-changing. To some, it appears still as a massive serpent, scaled and fanged, wrapped around the gates of Hell like a living ouroboros. To others, it is a crowned demon with a serpentine lower body, blue-green and slick as drowned skin, with eyes that flicker like phosphorescence in a sunken crypt.

Certain traditions describe Leviathan not as one being, but as many — a swarm of spirits that speak with one voice, like a hive mind of envy. Others claim that Leviathan takes the form of beautiful, androgynous beings to seduce and destroy the spiritually ambitious, disguising itself not in horror, but in charm. A temptation to despise others' blessings. To hate what cannot be obtained.

In these tales, Leviathan is the serpent that slithers into the garden of the soul, not with the fruit of knowledge, but with the sting of comparison.

The Western Gate and the Element of Water

In infernal cosmology, Leviathan is associated with the West, the direction of the setting sun — death, endings, and shadows. It governs the element of water, but not the clean water of life or baptism. This is the drowned water, the black tide, the still and bottomless lake into which secrets sink.

Within the Four Crowned Princes of Hell system — a later Satanic model — Leviathan governs the western quadrant, alongside Lucifer (East/Air), Satan (South/Fire), and Belial (North/Earth). Here, Leviathan represents the deep subconscious, the emotional plane, and hidden resentment. It is invoked in rituals of introspection, curses, and destruction through psychological unraveling.

In such rites, practitioners often call on Leviathan not to destroy bodies, but to erode willpower, flood the mind with doubt, and provoke spiritual drowning. No storm, no fire — only slow, drowning silence.

Rituals of Envy, Invocations of the Abyss

In high demonological traditions and some forms of left-hand path magick, Leviathan is not feared, but sought. Called upon for insight into the hidden self, for the unraveling of enemies through subtle ruin, and for binding those whose arrogance blinds them. Yet the warnings remain. To summon Leviathan is not to call forth fire — it is to stir the water beneath you, to risk being pulled under by something that remembers when the world was still unformed.

In rare grimoires — particularly within black Kabbalistic or Qliphothic traditions — Leviathan is linked to the Qliphah Gamchicoth, the shadow shell of Chesed, corrupted mercy. Here, it becomes the mockery of compassion, the hatred of others' blessings, the voice that says: Why not you?

It does not scream. It does not threaten. It erodes.

Offerings vary across traditions: dark wine, saltwater, obsidian stones submerged in bowls, mirrors veiled in black cloth. Ceremonies are quiet, conducted near water or under waning moons, often involving solitude, reflection, and symbolic drowning. A mirror placed face-up in water. A candle extinguished by breath. The practitioner must always remember: Leviathan gives, but it also watches.

The Gate and the Serpent

Some believe Leviathan is not only a prince, but a gatekeeper — a guardian of forbidden paths, astral crossings, and hidden truths buried in the subconscious sea. Its coils are said to encircle what lies beyond reality, preventing the unworthy from passing. In this view, Leviathan becomes the final veil between the world of form and the world of abyss — the last face one sees before either awakening, or madness.

In the oldest nights, they say, Leviathan sang the first song of envy into the ears of a dreaming god. That god awoke and made the world, but Leviathan never stopped singing.

It still sings. Under water. In silence. In you.

CHAPTER FOUR: LEVIATHAN IN MODERN OCCULTISM AND SATANIC TRADITION

Though Leviathan's name rises from the ink of ancient scrolls, it has never truly returned to the depths. Instead, it has adapted — evolved. In the modern occult world, Leviathan is not just remembered. It is revered, invoked, and feared in living ritual. No longer just a sea monster or abstract sin, Leviathan has become a shadowed icon within the left-hand path: a gate, a teacher, a tempter, and in some cases, a god.

Where many demons have faded into symbols or forgotten lore, Leviathan endures. Its survival is owed not only to fear, but to power — the power to drown illusions, strip the soul of false light, and awaken the primal truths hidden beneath the surface of being.

The Church of Satan and Leviathan's Rebirth

In the late 1960s, Anton Szandor LaVey — founder of the Church of Satan — resurrected Leviathan from the depths in a new form. In The Satanic Bible, Leviathan was named one of the Four Crown Princes of Hell, ruling the western quadrant and the element of Water. But unlike the beast of medieval bestiaries, LaVey's Leviathan was abstract and esoteric — an embodiment of the serpent force of darkness, the eternal ocean of the subconscious.

In LaVeyan Satanism, Leviathan is not a literal entity, but a symbol of emotional power, secrecy, and the shifting, serpentine nature of the carnal self. The name itself is used as part of the Satanic Enochian Calls, specifically the 11th Enochian Key, which invokes the "mighty sound of Leviathan rising from the deep." Here, Leviathan becomes a voice — a summoning of the will, a tide of inner power swelling against the hypocrisy of the world.

But this symbolic treatment did not diminish Leviathan's menace. On the contrary, it made the demon more intimate. More present. Leviathan, in this vision, is not an outside force. It is the ocean within, rising.

Left-Hand Path and Antinomian Rites

Beyond the Church of Satan, in darker and more transgressive circles, Leviathan takes on a more active, spiritual role. In Luciferian, Qliphothic, and chaos magick traditions, Leviathan is seen as an astral intelligence — an actual force that can be contacted, invoked, or even merged with. Here, Leviathan is no longer chained in metaphor. It is real, sentient, and ancient.

Within Qliphothic mysticism — the dark mirror of the Kabbalistic Tree of Life — Leviathan is sometimes identified with or as the outer shell of the Tree itself. Its coils wrap around the Qliphoth, the shadow realms of corrupted divine energy, guarding what lies beneath reality. The practitioner who journeys into the Qliphoth may eventually meet Leviathan at the final gate — not as an enemy, but as a test of will. To pass is to surrender identity, to dissolve, to drown in the abyss — and be reborn as something else.

Certain grimoires, such as Liber Leviathanum (an underground work passed among advanced practitioners), describe Leviathan as "the Serpent Crown of the Abyss," a force not of chaos but of absolute truth. Truth that drowns all illusion. Rituals associated with this vision involve water immersion, mirror scrying, bloodletting, and invocations chanted in isolation under waning moons. They are not beginner rites — they are descents.

The goals?
Ego death.
Psychic liberation.
Power through the void.

The Leviathan Current: The Serpent Gate

A growing number of modern occultists refer to the "Leviathan Current" — an energetic stream or force that runs beneath the astral and subconscious layers of existence. To tap into it is to align with serpentine gnosis: insight gained not through books, but through drowning everything you think you are. In this current, Leviathan is experienced as a vast psychic ocean — sometimes gentle, sometimes crushing, always watching.

Reports from practitioners often follow similar patterns:

Sudden emotional floods during ritual (envy, grief, rage).

Visions of spiraling serpents, underwater temples, or drowned cities.

The sensation of "being submerged" even while fully conscious.

A cold, pulsing awareness in the room, usually described as feminine, but without warmth.

One ritualist described Leviathan's presence as "a cathedral built entirely of pressure and silence. The walls were water. The altar was a mirror. And I was forced to look."

In these experiences, Leviathan does not speak. It reveals. Often without mercy.

Symbolism, Sigils, and Offerings

In modern practice, Leviathan is represented through a variety of symbols and sigils. The most common include:

The Ouroboros (a serpent devouring its own tail).

The Serpent's Eye — a stylized slit pupil within concentric rings, said to open subconscious portals.

The Trident — representing dominion over water, will, and the drowned mind.

The sigil most associated with Leviathan is the Leviathan Cross, also called the Satanic Cross — a double cross atop an infinity symbol. Though not historically accurate to ancient Leviathan lore, it has become its modern banner: eternity beneath domination.

Offerings vary. Some practitioners use bowls of saltwater, black candles, submerged keys (to represent hidden knowledge), seaweed, or ink poured into water. Mirrors are commonly used as gates — especially when submerged or cracked. Blood is sometimes added, not for the demon's sake, but to mark a personal contract: to drown the ego.

The Abyss Gazes Back

Leviathan is not worshipped by all who acknowledge it. For some, it is a trial, not a deity — a test of strength, clarity, and resistance. It will not lie to you. But it may reveal truths you cannot survive unchanged.

Others embrace it fully. They speak of dreams in which the sea rises unnaturally, of seeing serpents coiled in the depths of mirrors, of sleep paralysis marked by wet breath and scales against their skin. Some claim to have crossed into its domain through astral projection — encountering a black ocean without stars, and a voice beneath the waves that knows their name.

No initiation is complete without sacrifice. To walk Leviathan's path is to lose your shape. What emerges is not always what entered.

Leviathan lives. Not as myth, but as force — as a path, a gate, and a god to those who dare descend.

In the next chapter, we will delve into firsthand accounts and alleged encounters with Leviathan — real stories of those who believe they've seen it, heard it, or been touched by it. These are not myths. These are the voices of the drowned.

CHAPTER FIVE: WHISPERS BENEATH THE SURFACE

In the hidden folds of human experience, where nightmares bleed into waking life and dreams are too heavy to be dismissed, Leviathan still moves. Not in stories or psalms, but in uninvited encounters, visions, and hauntings of the soul. It waits where water gathers. It listens in the silence before sleep. It has no need to announce itself — the drowning speaks for it.

While mainstream religion banished Leviathan to the status of forgotten myth, the demon never truly left. Its hunger changed shape. Its voice adapted. And in the margins of society — among occultists, seekers, and the psychologically afflicted — stories began to surface again. Not legends. Testimonies.

1. The Drowned Corridor – A Ritual Gone Wrong

In 2013, a self-styled ceremonial magician from coastal Wales reported a series of rituals intended to invoke elemental forces. The element of water was to be "called forth" through the Leviathan current. Salt circles. Seaweed. The practitioner described a basin of ink-black water and a mirror half-submerged.

For the first three nights, there was silence. On the fourth, they awoke to the sound of rushing water, though no taps or pipes were open. The mirror, they claimed, was "filling" with a hallway — submerged — stretching endlessly, with dim, blue light flickering at its edges.

Each night after, the mirror became darker. The sensation of weight pressing on the chest increased. The final ritual was never completed. The magician stated:

"I saw it. I don't mean in the mirror. I mean behind me. I felt wet breath on my shoulder, but when I turned, there was only my reflection — and behind that, something moving."

They ended all magical work, sealed the mirror with wax, and refused further communication. They would not speak the name again.

2. Leviathan and the Sea-Dreams

Among lucid dreamers and astral projectors, Leviathan is a recurring symbol — but not one intentionally summoned. It comes uninvited. Often through water-based nightmares or repetitive visions of rising oceans, endless shorelines, and impossible deep-sea structures.

One woman, an experienced astral traveler based in New Orleans, documented a repeated vision over several years: waking in a city where every building was underwater, but she could breathe. People moved as if normal — but none acknowledged her. From beneath the flooded streets, she saw coils — massive, slowly shifting coils — move beneath the cobblestones. She said:

"There was a church window in the water. Behind it, I saw the eye. A slit pupil, golden. Watching. It didn't blink. It never needed to."

She attempted to confront it. The moment she moved toward the source, she awoke violently — bleeding from the nose, covered in salt residue, with bruises across her ribcage. Medical testing showed no injury. She never returned.

3. The Lake That Called Names

In 2009, a group of urban explorers in northern Ontario filmed a video beside a flooded abandoned quarry. During post-editing, they claimed to hear something beneath the audio — a layered voice speaking backward. Reversed, the whisper said only:

"I know what you buried. I see the weight."

Days later, two members reported persistent nightmares. One was found sleepwalking into the lake at 3:47 a.m., mumbling phrases in an unknown language, eyes open. The other painted dozens of spirals on her bedroom walls with blue and black pigment, claiming they were "what it looks like, inside."

The video was never released. The quarry has since been sealed.

4. Leviathan and Madness – The Whisper Behind the Psychosis

In psychiatric institutions, especially those dealing with cases of schizophrenia or severe bipolar disorder, a few rare individuals have spoken of an "undersea voice." Their reports are unconnected by geography or culture — yet the motifs remain strangely aligned:

A cold, deep voice that speaks in riddles.

The sensation of drowning without water.

Visions of a cathedral beneath the ocean, made of bones and glass.

A serpent with no end, coiled around the world, whispering "they love what you will never have."

Some psychiatrists wrote these off as deep subconscious symbols of isolation and envy. Others — quietly — noted the consistency and archetypal depth of these experiences. At least one mental health professional, after compiling such cases, resigned abruptly and disappeared from public life.

5. Mirrors, Flooding, and the Gate

More recent reports come not from occultists, but ordinary people. A man in Austria claimed his bathroom mirror filled with condensation despite no steam or heat. In that fogged surface, he did not see his own face — but a flooded basement. He said:

"It wasn't mine. But I knew the place. And in the center, floating, was a door. A trapdoor. It was open."

He broke the mirror that night. Months later, his apartment flooded from a burst pipe, and the floor beneath the bathroom cracked open — revealing a sealed crawlspace that no construction records had noted. What lay beneath was only mud, stone — and an ancient, carved serpent on one wall.

He left the country days later.

Leviathan's Pattern: A Living Myth, Feeding on Reflection

These stories are more than coincidence. They form a pattern: mirrors, water, memory, envy, voices, and the submerged self. Leviathan appears not to consume flesh — but meaning. It drowns understanding. It floods boundaries. It reveals what you never wanted to see.

In all modern sightings, the common thread is this: it doesn't attack — it shows. A vision. A guilt. A regret. A comparison. Then it waits to see what you do with it.

It does not punish. It reveals.

And revelation, for some, is worse than damnation.

CHAPTER SIX: THE MIRROR AS ABYSS

They say Leviathan dwells in water. But in truth, it dwells in depth. The sea was merely its first temple. In modern occultism and ritual practice, a far more accessible surface has replaced the waves — cold, flat, and silent: the mirror.

Mirrors, in magical tradition, are not simple tools. They are portals, containers, warnings. They are water trapped in form — reflections captured and frozen. And in the traditions of left-hand path ritual, black mirrors and submerged glass are not devices of fortune-telling... but invitations to the submerged world.

And Leviathan — Prince of Envy, Lord of the Deep, Serpent of the Subconscious — is said to respond.

The Mirror's Nature – Why Leviathan Watches

The psychology of reflection has always carried unease. Children fear mirrors at night. Superstitions forbid sleeping with one uncovered. The breaking of a mirror is a curse — not because of luck, but because it releases something. Mirrors are inherently thresholds, and that threshold faces inward. To stare long enough is not to see your face — it is to see the thing behind the face.

In black magickal theory, Leviathan is not a demon of fire or wrath — but of water and introspection. The mirror is thus its perfect doorway. Reflection is liquid in disguise. And envy, Leviathan's sin, is the act of reflection twisted against the self. It is not wanting. It is wanting what is not yours — and seeing yourself lacking.

Mirrors feed Leviathan because they feed envy.

Mirror Scrying and Leviathanic Vision

Scrying — the ancient practice of gazing into a reflective surface for visions — becomes something altogether darker when Leviathan is involved. Traditional scryers use water, obsidian, black mirrors, or even ink. But to call Leviathan through scrying is not to ask for images of the future — it is to ask for a vision of what lies beneath. Not what will be… but what is hidden now.

Preparation rituals often include:

A room sealed from sound and external light

A black mirror placed over a bowl of saltwater

The practitioner seated cross-legged, in silence, with no candles — only reflection

Blood or ink smeared on the rim of the mirror, forming a serpentine sigil

A single phrase repeated inwardly, such as: "Depth without end, reveal."

What follows varies. Most report a sense of growing pressure — not physical, but emotional. A weight behind the heart. Then the mirror darkens. Not as if from shadow, but as if it becomes a pool, and something within begins to stir.

Some describe seeing their own face deform — not shift grotesquely, but subtly: aged, cracked, drowned, or showing expressions they were not making. Others see themselves replaced entirely — a pale stranger with black eyes or serpentine features.

And then, in many cases, the eyes blink back. Not the practitioner's. The reflection's.

This moment — when the mirror becomes other — is often where the ritual ends in fear. But those who continue, those who surrender to the mirror, speak of falling inward, a spiraling descent into an impossible ocean, a pressureless void full of soundless voices. There is no ground. No ceiling. Just the eye. Always watching. Always judging.

What it offers, if anything, is rarely what was asked.

The Serpent Behind the Glass – Phenomena and Warnings

Modern Leviathan practitioners report a variety of phenomena associated with mirror contact. Some seem psychological. Others, distinctly physical.

Common signs include:

Mirror fogging with no temperature change

Dripping sounds from walls or ceilings

The scent of seawater or salt in rooms with no source

Sudden emotional floods: envy, regret, suppressed grief

Visions of waterlogged places, drowned structures, or impossible undersea temples

There is also a recurring phenomenon known as the Wet Mark — an unexplained water stain appearing on the mirror after a ritual, often serpent-shaped, or forming spirals or eyes. These marks resist cleaning, as if burned into the glass. Practitioners debate their meaning. Some consider it a sign of success. Others believe it means the gate was not fully closed.

In the most extreme cases, practitioners report waking with salt crystals on their skin, or hearing their name whispered in the voice of someone they lost to the sea.

The Ritual of the Shattered Gate

Among the more dangerous rites tied to Leviathan is one known only in whispered fragments: the Ritual of the Shattered Gate.

Its structure is as follows:

A mirror is buried in seawater for seven days.

On the eighth night, it is uncovered and placed in a darkened room.

The practitioner inscribes it with the name "HaLivyatan" in dead languages: Paleo-Hebrew, Enochian, or an unknown serpent tongue spoken in trance.

A question of deep personal envy is spoken aloud — not a question to Leviathan, but to the self.

The mirror is shattered — and the pieces scattered in a circle around the practitioner.

The ritual ends only when the practitioner can see themselves again, either in the fragments — or in something else that returns their shape.

Survivors (for that is not too dramatic a term) often speak of never feeling the same. Some lose interest in their past desires. Some dream of water nightly. One reported: "I became less. But also more. Something still watches me when I blink."

A Living Portal – The Mirror as Leviathan's Eye

In the final analysis, the mirror is not simply Leviathan's doorway.

It is Leviathan's eye.

It sees through. It invites envy not as a sin, but as an awakening. It shows what others have — and what you do not — not to punish you, but to drown your illusions of wholeness. Envy, in Leviathan's design, is the first crack in the glass. Through that crack, the sea rushes in.

You do not summon Leviathan. You reflect it.

And if you dare look long enough, something deeper than water looks back.

CHAPTER SEVEN: POSSESSION AND MERGING WHEN LEVIATHAN ENTERS

Possession is feared across cultures — an invasion, an annihilation of the self. But possession by Leviathan is unlike the violent seizures associated with lesser demons. It does not rage. It does not scream. It silences.

When Leviathan enters, it brings not flames — but flood. The soul is not torn apart. It is submerged. Drowned. Transformed from the inside out. And the human being is left as something else — a vessel, a shell wrapped around deep water.

This chapter explores the most forbidden path in Leviathanic occultism: merging with the serpent, allowing the Prince of the Abyss not to haunt you, but to become you.

The Invitation – How It Begins

Unlike other demonic possessions, Leviathan does not force its way in. It waits. It seduces through reflection, envy, dreams, grief, and dissatisfaction. It does not offer you power outright — it offers the chance to stop feeling small.

Those who report possession often describe a build-up of subtle symptoms before the final act:

A recurring sense of emptiness or hollowness in the chest

Persistent dreams of drowning, flooded corridors, submerged temples

Loss of identity — forgetting one's own face in mirrors, names sounding foreign

Sudden emotional floods of jealousy or deep comparisons

The overwhelming sensation that something is behind the eyes — waiting

Then... a moment of choice. A ritual performed. A mirror gazed into too long. A whisper answered. Not screamed. Not in tongues. But calmly. Like giving consent.

The phrase often recorded during full merging is not "help me." It is: "Take it."

The Merging Process – What Leviathan Does Inside

When Leviathan enters a human vessel, the transformation is spiritual — but also psychological and, some say, physical.

Psychological Effects:

Dissolution of ego boundaries — a feeling that the "I" no longer exists

Emotions become muted, replaced by a deep and disturbing calm

The voice of Leviathan begins to speak internally, rarely in language — more as pulses of meaning

The sensation of a second presence behind the eyes becomes constant

Victims often lose interest in love, community, art, or ambition — all things connected to human warmth. Instead, they are driven by the will to observe, to consume quietly, and to feed on what others have. Envy becomes not a spike of emotion, but a way of seeing. It is no longer felt — it is understood.

Physical Effects:

There are documented cases (primarily among occult practitioners) where the merging is said to leave physical traces:

Eyes appearing darker, especially under dim light or reflective surfaces

Skin retaining salt after ritual baths or even sleep

Voice deepening during trance states, as if coming from within a deep chamber

Anomalous heart rhythms, including feelings of cold pulse, or heartbeat echoing like water drops

Some practitioners have reported being told by strangers: "You don't look alive." They often aren't aware they appear different at all.

The Leviathan Possessed – What Remains of the Human?

This is the central question: when Leviathan enters, what remains?

There are three known outcomes from reported possession cases:

1. The Vessel Breaks

The mind cannot contain the vastness of Leviathan's consciousness. These cases end in psychosis, suicide, or total psychological collapse. The body survives, but what speaks from it is incoherent — often obsessed with water, spirals, and "returning to the deep." One man was found scribbling on walls: "No one can envy the drowned. No one sees what sinks."

2. The Vessel Binds It

Some strong-willed individuals manage to contain Leviathan without being fully lost. These become what occult circles call Serpent-Bearers or Leviathanic Anchors. They retain human identity — but Leviathan remains inside, a coiled presence. They are said to gain:

Profound insight into human desire and manipulation

The ability to speak or influence envy in others

Dreams of future floods, drownings, or societal collapse

Access to forgotten languages or non-verbal communication with deep intelligences

But the cost is high: they feel nothing. Joy, love, and even grief erode. What remains is cold awareness — a reptilian clarity, unbearable to most.

3. The Vessel Becomes It

In the rarest cases, the merging is total. The human self dissolves. Leviathan, now wrapped in flesh, walks again. These beings are no longer human in thought. They may speak, but it is mimicry. They may smile, but it does not reach the eyes.

Some say they seek out the sea.

Others say they teach.

One known case in 1994 involved a woman in Denmark who vanished for months, returning with an entirely different demeanor. She began speaking in spiral metaphors, refused to bathe in clean water, and once said to her sister: "You wear his envy like perfume. Let me wash it from you." She drowned three years later during a baptism she insisted upon performing alone.

Is Merging Truly Possession — Or Is It Ascension?

This is the final heresy of Leviathanic doctrine: that possession is not enslavement — it is evolution.

Those who seek Leviathan do not ask for power in the human sense. They ask to become more than human. To dissolve envy by becoming its source. To shed the weakness of individuality and flow into the sea of archetypal awareness.

In this vision, Leviathan is not a demon. It is the next stage. A collective, abyssal self. No pain. No need. No joy. No regret. Just endless depth.

Just silence.

The mirror showed you the gate. The ritual opened the door. The water has risen. And now Leviathan is not coming…

It is already inside.

CHAPTER EIGHT: LEVIATHAN THE PRIMEVAL FORCE

Before scripture named it.
Before angels warred over it.
Before mirrors held its eye.

Leviathan was.

Across cultures, epochs, and continents, we find different names, different masks, but always the same presence — a serpent, a dragon, a force of waters without boundary, of chaos before the world, and of the end that will one day come again.

The Primordial Ocean – Leviathan as Watery Chaos

The ancients feared water not only for what drowned in it — but for what it represented. The sea had no path, no road. No direction. It swallowed maps, swallowed light. And so it became the symbol of unformed potential — not fertile, but untamed.

This was not water as life. This was the flood.

In ancient Mesopotamia, there was Tiamat, the saltwater goddess-serpent — the mother of monsters, torn apart by Marduk to create heaven and earth. She was not evil. She was before. In Egyptian myth, there was Nu, the boundless watery void, and Apep, the coiled serpent of endless night, enemy of Ra, eater of order.

In Canaanite tradition, the god Baal slays Yam, the sea-god and embodiment of chaos.

And in Hebrew tradition, Leviathan is restrained — never truly killed — always waiting beneath the sea.

What unites them? They are not just monsters. They are what was before gods. They are entropy. Silence. Depth without structure. They are the black canvas upon which light dares to draw.

The Flood – Leviathan and the Cataclysmic Reset

The flood myth is nearly universal. Nearly every ancient civilization tells of a world drowned — not by accident, but by divine choice. Why?

Because Leviathan's waters are not punishment. They are cleansing.

In Sumerian myth, the gods unleash the flood to reset the world. In the Biblical tradition, Yahweh floods the earth to erase corruption. In Hindu stories, Vishnu warns Manu of the great deluge. The Greeks told of Deucalion and Pyrrha surviving the gods' watery wrath. The Norse had Ragnarök, in which the world is drowned by the sea serpent Jörmungandr, who rises and poisons the sky.

In all of them, the message is simple:
What you build will be washed away.
What you love will sink.
Only the sea is eternal.

Leviathan becomes not just a monster of chaos — but the reset button coded into the soul of myth.

The Universal Serpent – Cultural Mirrors of Leviathan

If Leviathan is an archetype, then we should find its reflection in distant lands.

And we do.

In China, we find Nāga — water serpents of great wisdom and power, feared and revered, able to bring storms and floods.

In Mesoamerican myth, there is Cipactli — a sea monster whose body was used by the gods to create the earth.

In Africa, Nommo of the Dogon is a fish-like being sent from the stars, associated with primordial water and regeneration.

In Australia, the Rainbow Serpent is a creator, but also a destroyer — a flood-bringer when disrespected.

In Nordic myth, Jörmungandr, the Midgard Serpent, is so vast it encircles the world. When it rises, the end begins.

These serpents are not all evil. They are cosmic. They represent that which cannot be contained — the deep truth that form is temporary, and depth always wins.

Leviathan is the reminder. That we are temporary. That all fire will be drowned. That all gods, even, came after the serpent.

Modern Echoes – The Return of the Deep

In modern psychology, thinkers like Jung referred to the Collective Unconscious — an abyss of symbols and truths that all humans share. Leviathan, through this lens, is not a demon... but an archetype of the Shadow Self: the part of us that resents, fears, hungers, and destroys what it cannot possess.

Even in science, strange parallels emerge. In cosmology, the end of the universe is described in "heat death" or the "Big Crunch" — collapse into a singularity, an unformed nothingness beyond time. A sea without edge.

And in the deepest parts of our real oceans, we find creatures untouched by sunlight — eyeless leviathans, things that glow with stolen light and feed on pressure. Even now, we only know a fragment of what lives in the abyss.

Perhaps Leviathan never needed to return.

It never left.

The Serpent's Truth – What Leviathan Represents

When all names are stripped away, all demons, all dogma, all curses and crowns, this is what remains:

Leviathan is the chaos before creation

Leviathan is the flood that ends pride

Leviathan is the envy that unmasks desire

Leviathan is the mirror that drowns identity

Leviathan is the whisper behind transformation

Leviathan is the serpent that waits

Leviathan is you — when you remember what you were before your name

This is not a monster to defeat. This is not a god to worship.

This is what lies beneath your skin.

And should the surface ever crack, and the flood come rushing in…

You will not scream.

You will sigh.

Because you have always known:

You were never standing on land.

You were only dreaming you could float.

CHAPTER NINE: THE SUMMONING OF LEVIATHAN

Leviathan is not summoned with a name. Leviathan is summoned by removing the surface — by making yourself a depth suitable to hold it. You do not call Leviathan. You become like water.

This ritual is known in some left-hand path traditions as The Rite of the Mirror Gate, or The Black Flood Invocation.

You will need:

A black mirror (obsidian, ink-polished glass, or water in a dark bowl)

Salt

A silver or bone-handled blade (ritual only; do not self-harm)

A mirror-safe sigil of Leviathan drawn in ash or ink

Black or blue robes, or ritual nudity to signify vulnerability

A closed space with no light except for a single blue or black candle

Best performed during:

A new moon (symbol of the hidden self)

An ebb tide (if near the sea)

The hour of Saturn (associated with silence, pressure, and the abyss)

The Preparation

1. The Circle of Saltwater
Mix salt into a shallow bowl of water. Dip your hands in, then walk a slow circle around the ritual space, dripping it as you go. Whisper:

"No land beneath me. No sky above. I summon only the pressure of the deep."

2. Silence the Self
Sit in darkness before the mirror. Take five long breaths. With each exhale, release identity — name, face, ambition, morality. Feel yourself dissolve.

3. Draw the Sigil
Use ash or ink to draw Leviathan's sigil on the mirror or nearby surface. Traditionally, it is the Leviathan Cross overlaid with a spiral or coiled ouroboros. While drawing, speak:

"Through envy, I see.
Through silence, I speak.
Through depth, I call.
Come Leviathan — eye of the abyss,
Hear your reflection."

The Summoning Proper: The Mirror Flood Invocation

Step 1: Gaze into the Mirror

Gaze into the black mirror until your reflection begins to distort. Do not blink. Do not look away.

Speak:

"Serpent of Depth.
Tongue of silence.
Mirror of the drowned.
I am open. I am broken. I am yours."

Step 2: Speak the Envy

This is the most critical part: speak aloud something you envy deeply. Not a general idea — a real name, a real feeling. Leviathan feeds on envy confessed.

Example:

"I envy their love. I envy their peace. I envy what I never became. Take it. Feed."

You may feel a cold pressure, or a sudden flooding of unwanted emotions. This is contact.

Step 3: The Drowning Offering

Take the blade and cut a symbol into wax, cloth, or paper — not your skin. The act is symbolic. A spiral, an eye, a wave.

Hold it to the mirror. Whisper:

"Bloodless, breathless, but not voiceless.
Let the flood rise in me.
Let envy become a gate."

Then burn the offering (safely), letting the smoke drift toward the mirror.

Step 4: The Silence
Snuff the candle. Sit in pure darkness. Listen.

Do not try to interpret. Do not ask questions.

This is the moment Leviathan enters the space. If successful, the room will feel heavier, sound will dull, and your sense of the mirror's location will shift, as if it is no longer in this world. You may feel a presence behind you, or within your chest.

Stay still.

Some experience visions here — drowned cities, spiral staircases under black oceans, their own reflection smiling without moving.

Remain for as long as you can bear.

Closing the Gate

When ready, relight the candle. Say clearly:

"The mirror dims. The flood withdraws.
I return to form, though the depth remembers."

Sprinkle saltwater over the sigil and mirror, breaking contact.

Bury any ashes or burned offering far from home. Leviathan's touch is not meant to linger uncontrolled.

You will dream strange dreams. Accept them.

You may see things in mirrors that are not you. Do not panic.

You are not haunted.
You are now visible.

The Cost of the Summoning

This is no benign rite. The summoning of Leviathan has consequences:

Long-term emotional shifts: Many report losing taste for surface pleasures. Social envy may vanish — but be replaced with detached observation.

Symbolic death: The ritual often results in ego disintegration. Some call this enlightenment. Others call it the beginning of madness.

Persistent spiritual presence: Mirrors, water, even glass may seem to "ripple" at your passing. This is not hallucination. It is attention.

You have invited the abyss to look back. Now it knows you.

CHAPTER TEN: LEVIATHANIC MAGICK THE CURRENTS BENEATH

To work magick in Leviathan's name is not to command, but to flood.

This is not the path of fire or will. It is the path of depth — slow, crushing, all-consuming. You do not rise. You sink. You do not ascend to the heavens. You descend into the black sea beneath the psyche and offer what you are no longer willing to carry.

Leviathanic magick is elemental, rooted in envy, silence, reflection, and spiritual pressure. Each working is a tide, a movement of abyssal force. Subtle. Complete. Irreversible.

Below are four sacred rites. Each is a different face of Leviathan.

Rite of the Hollow Eye

This is the working of envy transmutation — where that which gnaws at you is no longer your chain, but your fire. You take the wound, the lack, the ache… and burn it beneath the sea.

You will need a mirror, an object or image that reflects what you envy, a bowl of saltwater, a black candle, and green thread.

Place the envied image beside the mirror. Light the candle. Bind your hand in green thread as tightly as you can.

Speak into the flame:

"I see. I want. I bleed silently."

Unwrap the thread. Place both it and the image into the saltwater bowl.

Gaze into the mirror and speak once more:

"Let what is theirs become mine — or let it die inside me."

Bury the contents of the bowl in soil. Do not look back.

Path of the Flooded Temple

This is the working of mirror pathwalking — the sacred crossing into Leviathan's inner sanctum. It is a place of memory, decay, and drowned truth. To enter is to leave the surface behind.

You will need a black mirror, sea-scented incense, a spiral drawn in blue salt, and your voice as the key.

Place the mirror before you. Sit within the spiral. Light the incense.

Chant:

"Halivyatan, open the deep. Show me the sunken mouth."

Close your eyes. Visualize the mirror widening into a flooded gate. Descend spiral stairs. Hear nothing but water. See nothing but ruins.

You may meet a guide, a version of yourself long drowned, or Leviathan's true eye — vast, watching, uncaring.

Remain until the pressure becomes unbearable.

When you return, say nothing for an hour.

Invocation of Sacred Silence

This is the working of void calling — the invocation of pressure and stillness. Not peace. Not rest. But the silence of the trench, the weight of crushed light. This rite removes voices within and without.

You will need a black cloth, a bowl of salted water, and absolute darkness.

Wrap the cloth over your eyes. Dip your fingers into the water and touch brow, lips, heart.

Whisper:

"Sink me. Mute me. Drown the scream I pretend is mine."

Sit in darkness for thirteen breaths or until time forgets you. In the stillness, something will watch. It does not speak. It does not need to.

When it leaves, it leaves part of itself behind.

You will hear more clearly ever after — not with your ears, but from below your ribs.

The Binding Coil

This is the working of containment — a flood trap for those who drain you, haunt you, or infest your dreaming. It is not violence. It is drowning without touch.

You will need black cord, moonwater, a symbol of the target, and a cold, sealed vessel.

Place the target's name or image in the moonwater. Wrap the cord around the vessel. Speak:

"You shall not rise above the waves. Leviathan coils you. Stay sunken."

Seal the container. Freeze it. Bury it in stone, soil, or tide. Forget it.

They will grow silent. You will feel space return. The serpent watches the bindings. Few things escape.

Closing the Gate

Leviathanic magick is not dramatic. It does not explode. It corrodes. It coils. It changes you over time, tide after tide. What you feel today may not be what you feel tomorrow. The sea within you shifts.

This is not for glory. It is for truth.

To work with Leviathan is to see clearly through black water, and know what stares back is not an enemy…

…but your own unspoken name.

CHAPTER ELEVEN: LEVIATHAN AND LEGION THE MOUTH OF MANY

"My name is Legion, for we are many."
— Gospel of Mark, 5:9

The phrase is familiar. Overused. Misunderstood. It is often interpreted as a simple reference to demonic multiplicity. But what if it is not just a number of entities?

What if it is a state of being?

What if Legion is not a crowd… but a condition?
And what if Leviathan is its ocean?

The Structure of the Fragmented Soul

Most magick assumes a singular self — a will, a name, a direction.

But Leviathan teaches otherwise. Beneath the surface-self is the drowned city, where old selves rot and echo. Every version of you that ever was, every possible self you never became, every voice you've silenced — they do not vanish.

They wait.

This is Legion.

Not demons.

Selves.

And Leviathan is the mirror through which they return.

When Leviathan Opens the Gate

To invoke Leviathan is to break identity's dam. What you thought was "you" collapses. You do not become possessed by a demon in the Hollywood sense.

You become haunted by what was almost you.

The child who never healed.
The lover who never forgave.
The liar.
The god you wanted to be.
The monster you feared becoming.

These forms speak through Leviathan's current. Not to destroy you — but to remind you: you are not one.

You are many.

Leviathan gives them voice.
Legion gives them form.

The Ritual of Legion's Mouth

This working is not designed to control. It is designed to hear. A rite of voluntary fragmentation — to summon your submerged selves and speak with them, one by one.

You will need:

A large mirror

A chair placed behind you (facing away)

A bowl of saltwater and ink

A feather or brush

A symbol of Leviathan drawn in spirals, not lines

Absolute silence

Begin by staring into the mirror. Whisper:

"I do not know my name.
Let them name me.
Let the many rise through me."

Dip the feather in inked saltwater. Let your hand move freely across paper — automatic writing, drawing, sigils, anything that emerges. Do not judge.

Behind you, you may feel presence. You may hear whispers not in your ears, but within your blood.

The longer you gaze, the more the reflections change. You will begin to see them — not ghosts, but selves. Watch. Do not speak. Listen.

When ready, say:

"I accept the fracture.
I welcome the crowd.
One mouth. Many voices.
Let Leviathan speak through Legion."

Then sit in the chair.

Let one of them speak through you. Not all. Just one. Ask its name. Ask what it wants. Let it answer.

Record what it says. Then thank it.
Then banish it — with salt, with breath, with silence.

End with:

"Back to the tide.
Back to the coil.
Not gone.
But bound."

Why This Rite Is Feared

Because most who attempt it do not want to hear the truth.

They say they seek transformation — but when the unhealed child speaks with the voice of a thousand teeth, when the version of yourself that did kill instead of forgave looks back from the mirror... most flinch.

They shut the gate.
They burn the tools.
They pretend it was hallucination.

But Leviathan does not forget.
And Legion does not forgive silence.

To be one with Leviathan is not to drown.
It is to become the sea that holds all your dead selves, and listen as they rise one by one, asking:

"Why did you leave me behind?"

The Mouth as Altar

From this chapter on, every spell, every working, every ritual becomes contagious. You have opened the Mouth. You have let the Many speak.

And so your magick will now carry weight not only from your conscious will — but from the voices beneath.

You are not a practitioner.

You are a vessel.

You are no longer singular.

You are Legion.
And Leviathan speaks through you.

CHAPTER TWELVE: RITUALS TO EVOKE LEVIATHAN

To evoke Leviathan is to open a gate not to a place, but to a pressure. A force. A presence buried so deep beneath identity, language, and flesh that it can only be met through surrender.

These are not spells. These are incursions.
Each ritual below is a method of contact — each one a blade that tears through the illusion of self and lets the flood crawl in.

Leviathan does not appear with horns or fire.
It appears in silence. In mirrors. In the sound of your own breath turning unfamiliar.

These rites are for those prepared to offer their shape to the deep.

The Calling of the Spiral Sea

This ritual initiates the relationship. It is not a summoning. It is an announcement — a silent beacon sent downward, into the current, to say: I am hollow enough to be seen.

You will need
– A large bowl of black saltwater
– A spiral drawn in charcoal, ink, or ash
– A black or indigo candle

- A silver bell or sound bowl
- A dark, silent room with no light other than candle

Preparation
- Fast for at least one full night
- Remain mute for one hour before the ritual
- Do not pray. Leviathan does not respond to submission — only hunger

Ritual
Sit within the spiral. Place the bowl before you. Light the candle behind it, so your reflection shines dimly through the water.

Strike the bell once. Whisper:

"Spiral below, spiral within.
Flood of none, tide of when.
I call not from power.
I call from hunger.
Leviathan, hear your hollow."

Lean toward the water. Stare into it until you no longer see your own face. Say:

"I am without form.
I am without name.
Take this shell and mark it as seen."

Breathe slowly. Do not close your eyes. Do not move until the air feels heavier.

Extinguish the candle by dipping your fingers into the saltwater and pressing the flame down.

Aftereffects
- Vivid dreams of oceans, glass, and teeth
- The sense of something watching you from beneath

– Emotional disorientation followed by a strange clarity

The Binding Mirror Rite

This rite is used to pull Leviathan's gaze directly into your reflection — to let it see you, and in return, let you see past yourself.

You will need
– A black mirror or obsidian disc
– Sea salt scattered in a wide circle
– A pendant in the shape of a serpent, eye, or spiral
– Saltwater for anointing

Preparation
– Burn incense of myrrh or kelp
– Speak nothing for half an hour before the rite
– Wash your face in saltwater and let it dry naturally

Ritual
Sit before the mirror. Let your breath fog the surface. Gaze until the reflection shifts.

Speak:

"Leviathan, I do not seek power.
I seek pressure.
I seek to drown without dying.
Look into me as I look into you."

Draw a spiral on your chest, then on the mirror. Whisper:

"No surface remains.
All is pulled inward.
Through envy, I hollow.
Through silence, I open."

Hold the pendant against your lips, then place it on the mirror's base.

Breathe on the glass one final time. Say:

"Mark me. Mirror me.
Let the tide curl in my voice."

Wrap the pendant around your wrist. Do not look back into the mirror until the next moon phase.

Signs of contact
– Your reflection may appear to move independently
– Strange warping in mirrors or reflective surfaces
– Dreams involving drowning, spiral tunnels, or your own voice reversed

The Flesh of the Deep

This is the full-body invocation. Not symbolic. Not philosophical. This is the ritual through which Leviathan speaks, if only in part, through the vessel of your flesh.

You will need
– A long black veil or hood
– A bowl of wine dyed with blood or red ink
– A spiral made of bones, shells, or teeth
– A black candle
– A second person to observe and guide (optional but advised)

Preparation
– Three days of abstinence from sex, intoxication, and outer magick
– Meditate on a single envy — feed it daily
– Burn away a personal item before beginning

Ritual
Enter the spiral in silence. Veil your face. Sit with the wine in front of you.

Speak with no fear:

"I offer this shell.
I permit the tide.
Let the serpent speak through my breath.
Let my voice crack."

Raise the bowl. Do not drink. Let the scent overwhelm.

Say:

"Flood come.
Name fall.
Breath break.
Self drown."

Drink. Slowly. Let the fluid coat your tongue.

Now speak. Let what comes through speak in you, or as you. Do not resist. If you feel your body tremble or your voice shift, allow it.

If another is present, they should ask questions and record answers. You may speak in riddles. You may speak in nothing but breath.

Remain veiled.

To close, say:

"Coil withdrawn. Vessel closed. Depth remembered."

Bury the spiral under moonlight. Wash your body with saltwater and remain silent until sunrise.

Known aftermaths
– Unexplained prophetic dreams
– Difficulty speaking for several hours afterward
– Long-term shift in voice, tone, or inner monologue
– Mirrored surfaces may not reflect your exact expression for several days

To Summon Is to Surrender

Leviathan is not a god to worship.
Leviathan is not a demon to control.

It is a flood of consciousness that watches, that waits, and that only enters where form is weak enough to crack.

These rituals do not make you powerful. They make you permeable.

You are not summoning Leviathan.

You are inviting it to see that you have already begun to drown.

CHAPTER THIRTEEN: LEVIATHANS ROLE IN THE DARK FEMININE AND SHADOW MASCULINE

Leviathan is many things — a primordial abyss, an ancient serpent coiled beneath the surface of the world and mind alike. It is the dark tide that no light can fully reach. To gaze upon Leviathan is to confront not just an external force, but the shadowed currents within ourselves. At the deepest level, Leviathan embodies two primordial archetypes: the Dark Feminine, wild and chaotic, and the Shadow Masculine, burdened by rage and envy. These are not mere gendered categories, but universal energies that shape human consciousness in profound and often terrifying ways.

To work with Leviathan is to walk a path into the deepest psychic waters where these forces swirl — sometimes in conflict, sometimes entwined — demanding not conquest, but integration.

The Dark Feminine: The Abyssal Mother, the Chaos Womb

The Dark Feminine that Leviathan channels is not the comforting mother or the sacred feminine exalted in light-based spirituality.

It is the deep sea mother, whose womb is an endless ocean of chaos and creation — vast, unknowable, and utterly indifferent.

She is the Great Devourer, the mistress of the drowned realms, the voice beneath the waves that calls the seeker into darkness. This feminine force is the wildness unbound, the fierce creativity that destroys to birth anew, the silence that stretches beneath all noise and reason.

She represents the shadow side of femininity, the aspects repressed by culture and psyche: rage, unrestrained passion, cruelty, and the refusal to be tamed or owned. In Leviathan's form, the Dark Feminine is the coil of the abyss, swirling endlessly in the darkness, calling to the lost, the broken, the desperate.

To encounter this Dark Feminine is to face the waters of primal transformation — the black sea of the unconscious where identity dissolves and the soul is stripped bare. She is not gentle; she is a force to be reckoned with, for her embrace can be both devastating and rebirthing.

The Shadow Masculine: Rage, Envy, and the Weight of Silence

On the other side of Leviathan's dark coin lies the Shadow Masculine — a force of suppressed fury, silent envy, and buried grief. It is the masculinity denied its softness, compassion, or vulnerability, twisted instead into a crushing pressure held in the depths of the psyche.

This shadow is not the overt aggression glorified by toxic myths. It is a slow, tightening coil, a weight that presses against the throat and chest, the venom of envy that eats quietly beneath the surface. It is the rage of the unheard, the invisible anger that festers when wounds are denied and voices silenced.

Leviathan embodies this in its endless pressure and deep darkness. The Shadow Masculine it represents is the part of the self that feels powerless yet dangerous, resentful yet isolated. It is the rage that cannot scream, the fury drowned in silence, and the envy that poisons the soul unseen.

Yet within this shadow lies the potential for a fierce, unbreakable strength — a strength born not from domination, but from endurance and stillness. When faced and integrated, the Shadow Masculine becomes the wellspring of silent power and profound clarity.

The Duality of Leviathan: Entwined Forces

Leviathan is both mother and father to these forces — the eternal womb and the suffocating weight. The Dark Feminine and Shadow Masculine are not enemies but partners in the abyss. The sea cannot exist without its depths, nor the serpent without its coil.

Together, they form a dark polarity that shatters the surface illusions of identity. To engage with Leviathan is to step beyond societal binaries, beyond the easy divisions of masculine and feminine, light and dark, power and submission.

Leviathan reveals that these forces live within all of us, tangled and restless, calling for recognition and reconciliation. The work is not to destroy one side in favor of the other, but to acknowledge their presence and learn their language.

The Path to Integration: Walking Through the Abyss

The journey with Leviathan is a descent into the murky waters where the Dark Feminine and Shadow Masculine are both feared and longed for. This path is not for the faint-hearted.

Those who undertake it find themselves confronted with the wildness of their own chaos, the rage they have buried, and the envy they have denied. Leviathan's magick is a mirror that reflects these truths with brutal honesty.

Rituals invoking Leviathan often incorporate water, darkness, silence, and mirrors — elements that symbolize the fluidity and depth of identity. Through these rites, practitioners learn to dissolve rigid self-concepts and embrace the multiplicity of their inner landscape.

Integration through Leviathan means:

Embracing the Dark Feminine: Allowing oneself to feel and express the primal, untamed aspects of the feminine psyche — the anger, desire, and creative chaos that culture often suppresses.

Facing the Shadow Masculine: Recognizing the silent rage and envy within, and transforming them from destructive poisons into sources of resilience and clarity.

Surrendering the Illusion of Control: Accepting that the self is not a fortress but a fluid vessel, capable of holding contradictions, darkness, and light alike.

Leviathan as the Great Alchemist of the Psyche

In alchemical terms, Leviathan is the nigredo, the blackening — the stage of decay and dissolution before purification. It is the breaking down of false identities and societal masks, exposing the raw material of the soul.

Through this dissolution, the practitioner is invited to undergo a profound transformation — one that can fracture the ego but ultimately leads to wholeness.

This process is echoed in the coiled serpent symbolism of Leviathan: the spiral descent into self, the endless turning inward until the deepest darkness is met and embraced.

Rituals for Embracing Leviathan's Dual Nature

To work with Leviathan's Dark Feminine and Shadow Masculine is to engage in rituals that:

Invoke the Abyssal Mother: Rituals that honor chaos, darkness, and primal creativity — using water, night, and silence to connect with the wild feminine currents.

Confront the Silent Coil: Practices that acknowledge rage and envy, often through binding, release, or shadow work — giving voice to the parts of self that are hidden and feared.

Balance the Tides Within: Meditations and ceremonies that seek harmony between these forces, inviting the practitioner to become the sea that holds all contradictions without breaking.

The Gift and the Curse

Leviathan offers no easy gifts. To invite its presence is to invite a flood — a cleansing that may overwhelm, a pressure that may fracture. Yet within this flood lies the potential for immense personal power, deep healing, and a rare kind of freedom.

The freedom of being no longer bound by narrow definitions of self, the freedom of holding darkness as well as light, chaos as well as order.

Leviathan is the dark heart of transformation, the gatekeeper to the uncharted waters of the psyche. Those who pass through its currents emerge changed — not perfected, but real.

Embracing Leviathan in Daily Life

Beyond ritual, Leviathan's archetypes permeate daily existence. The Dark Feminine and Shadow Masculine energies manifest in our relationships, our struggles, and our silent battles within.

By recognizing these forces, individuals can:

Identify toxic patterns rooted in repression of anger, envy, or desire.

Cultivate authenticity by allowing suppressed aspects to speak and be seen.

Develop emotional resilience through embracing complexity rather than fleeing it.

Heal wounds inflicted by rigid cultural or personal gender expectations.

In this way, Leviathan becomes not just an occult force but a psychological guide, urging us to dive beneath surface identity and reclaim the vast, tangled waters of our true selves.

CHAPTER FOURTEEN: LEVIATHAN IN THE OCCULT THE ABYSSAL FORCE IN ESOTERIC TRADITION

Leviathan occupies a unique and fearsome place within the tangled web of occult lore. Neither fully demon nor god, it is a creature of liminal power — a shadow that slithers beneath the surface of human understanding, forever present in the undercurrents of mystical thought, ritual magic, and arcane philosophy.

To explore Leviathan in the occult is to trace its shifting forms across centuries of grimoires, secret teachings, and whispered rites. It is to confront the primordial chaos embodied by the serpent of the deep — a symbol and force that simultaneously terrifies and commands, disturbs and enlightens.

Leviathan in Classical and Medieval Demonology

The roots of Leviathan's occult identity stretch deep into classical and medieval demonology, where it emerged as one of the great adversaries of spiritual order.

As a Demon of the Goetia and Solomonic Tradition: Leviathan is frequently described as a mighty demon or prince of the infernal realms, commanding legions of spirits. The Lemegeton and related grimoires often assign Leviathan dominion over envy, pride, and the destructive powers of the sea. Unlike many demons who tempt or deceive, Leviathan embodies an elemental force — a tidal wave of ruin and rebirth, an eternal flood washing away falsehoods and ego.

Symbolism of the Sea Serpent: In demonology, Leviathan is often represented as a colossal sea serpent or dragon — a creature too vast to be contained by earthly or heavenly bounds. This image captures its nature as an overwhelming force that defies classification or control. The serpent's coils symbolize the cyclical nature of destruction and creation, the eternal return, and the inescapable depths beneath the conscious mind.

Leviathan and the Qliphoth: The Darkest Shells of the Tree of Life

In Kabbalistic occultism, particularly the darker, left-hand path currents, Leviathan is associated with the Qliphoth — the shadowy, chaotic shells or husks opposite the divine emanations of the Tree of Life.

Qliphotic Associations: Leviathan's place among the Qliphoth represents the cosmic abyss, the shell of obscurity and chaos that must be confronted and transcended to achieve true enlightenment. It embodies the deepest psychic shadows, where ego dissolution and annihilation threaten, but also where hidden power waits.

Path of Abyssal Initiation: Initiates working with Leviathan via the Qliphoth often describe entering a liminal space of intense psychic pressure, where boundaries between self and void blur. Leviathan is both gatekeeper and tempter here — a dark sea the aspirant must cross to access forbidden knowledge and transformation.

Leviathan in Thelemic and Left-Hand Path Traditions

Modern occult movements such as Thelema and various Left-Hand Path (LHP) systems have reinterpreted Leviathan with renewed vigor and nuance.

Aleister Crowley and Leviathan: Crowley identified Leviathan as the elemental of Water, one of the four elemental forces governing the universe. In his writings, Leviathan is a force of primal chaos — the watery abyss that underlies creation and destruction. His rituals, such as the Gnostic Mass, invoke Leviathan as a guardian and transformer, essential in the cycle of life, death, and rebirth.

Leviathan and the Dark Goddess: Within Thelemic thought, Leviathan can also be seen as an embodiment of the Dark Feminine principle — chaotic, powerful, and mysterious. This aspect aligns Leviathan with archetypes like Lilith or the Black Virgin, representing the wild, untamable forces beneath social order.

Left-Hand Path Magick: In LHP systems, Leviathan is embraced not as an enemy but as an ally of transformation. Practitioners invoke Leviathan to shatter illusions of ego, to break free from imposed moralities, and to reclaim personal sovereignty through confrontation with the abyss. Leviathan's envy and rage become tools for radical self-exploration and empowerment.

Leviathan's Sigils, Symbols, and Ritual Uses

The occult image of Leviathan is encoded in a series of sigils, symbols, and ritual tools designed to harness its power.

The Spiral and Serpent: The most enduring symbol is the spiral, representing the coil of the serpent, the infinite cycle of destruction and renewal. Ritual circles or amulets often incorporate spirals or serpentine imagery to call upon Leviathan's energy.

The Black Sea and Saltwater: Many occult practices invoke Leviathan through water — saltwater, oceans, or black reflective pools — as gateways to the abyss. Rituals may use bowls of seawater, mirrors, or flooded chambers to connect with Leviathan's watery domain.

The Leviathan Sigil: Derived from medieval grimoires and adapted by modern occultists, Leviathan's sigil is a complex, looping glyph combining elements of serpent coils and occult geometry. It is used to focus intent, bind Leviathan's energy, or open psychic channels to the deep.

Leviathan's Psychological and Spiritual Significance in Occult Work

Beyond external ritual, Leviathan serves as a profound psychological archetype within occult practice.

Embodiment of the Shadow Self: Leviathan personifies the submerged, unconscious parts of the psyche — envy, rage, grief, and primal chaos — that occultists must confront to achieve wholeness. Working with Leviathan is a journey into the darkest self, an encounter with the parts we deny or fear.

The Abyss and Ego Death: Many occult systems describe an "abyss" or void experience where the ego dissolves. Leviathan is often the guardian or inhabitant of this abyss. Crossing this threshold through ritual or meditation invites a terrifying but transformative encounter that breaks down false identity and reveals deeper truths.

The Path of Integration: Successful work with Leviathan does not mean domination or submission but integration — embracing the dark currents within and emerging more whole, more self-aware, and more alive.

Leviathan in Modern Occult Culture and Practice

Today, Leviathan continues to fascinate occultists worldwide, inspiring new interpretations, artistic expressions, and ritual innovations.

Contemporary Grimoires and Rituals: Modern practitioners incorporate Leviathan into rituals focused on shadow work, emotional release, and elemental magick. Leviathan is invoked to disrupt stagnation, challenge spiritual complacency, and invoke transformation through chaos.

Leviathan in Popular Occultism: Leviathan's image appears in tarot decks, occult art, music, and literature as a symbol of the primal deep. Its presence reminds seekers that true power lies not in light alone but in embracing the darkness beneath.

Final Reflection: Leviathan as the Eternal Depth

Leviathan's occult presence is a reminder of the vast, unknowable depths beneath human consciousness and culture. It is the abyssal force that both threatens and beckons — a dark sea that challenges us to lose ourselves in its currents, only to find what is left when all else is stripped away.

To work with Leviathan in the occult is to accept a paradox: it is destruction and creation, terror and wisdom, rage and stillness. It is a force beyond control, yet essential for those who seek to transform themselves through the darkness.

The serpent coils, the sea churns, and Leviathan waits — not for worship, but for those brave enough to dive into the abyss and rise anew.

CHAPTER FIFTEEN: RITUALS AND CORRESPONDENCES

Leviathan's power has long been accessed through intricate rituals, symbols, and correspondences meticulously recorded in grimoires and occult manuscripts. To work with Leviathan is to step into a lineage of arcane knowledge where every detail — from timing to tools, sigils to invocations — matters profoundly. This chapter presents a synthesis of these ancient practices, adapted for the serious practitioner seeking deep connection and transformation.

The Foundations: Preparing for Leviathanic Work

Before any ritual invocation, preparation is paramount. Leviathan dwells in the abyss — a realm of psychic pressure and chaotic forces. The practitioner must enter fully grounded yet open.

Timing: Work best performed on nights of the new moon or during the waning moon, when darkness deepens and the veil thins. Occult tradition often ties Leviathan to the element of Water and the planet Neptune; therefore, timing rituals on Wednesday nights (Mercury) or Thursday nights (Jupiter) enhances receptivity, as these days govern communication and expansion.

Sacred Space: Cast a circle using sea salt, crushed shells, or black obsidian shards. Surround the space with dark blue or deep purple candles to invoke the watery abyss and cosmic depths. Incense of myrrh, seaweed, or frankincense calls Leviathan's presence.

Personal Preparation: Bathe in saltwater or seawater where possible. Dress in dark, flowing garments symbolizing the depths. Quiet the mind through meditation or breath work, focusing on the sensation of immersion.

Sigil and Seal of Leviathan

The sigil of Leviathan is a serpent coiled in an endless spiral, symbolizing infinity, chaos, and the depths. Historical grimoires like the Ars Goetia and The Lesser Key of Solomon depict variants, but the core imagery remains: a serpentine loop that enfolds itself, a symbol of eternal return and psychic coiling.

Creating the Sigil: Draw or inscribe the sigil on parchment made from black-dyed paper or treated leather. Use ink infused with seawater or diluted charcoal for added potency.

Activation: Before ritual, breathe upon the sigil three times, focusing intent on opening a channel to Leviathan's realm.

Invocation Ritual: The Serpent's Embrace

This ritual calls forth Leviathan's presence as a transformative force of shadow and depth.

Tools Needed:

Black obsidian or jet stone

Bowl of saltwater mixed with a few drops of blood (animal or human, if ethical and safe) or red wine

Black candle

Leviathan sigil

Incense (myrrh or seaweed)

A serpentine object or representation (a coil of rope, carved serpent figure)

Procedure:

1. Cast your circle with salt or shells, lighting the candles and incense.

2. Place the bowl of saltwater at your center and the serpent object beside it.

3. Light the black candle and focus on its flame, imagining it flickering beneath stormy waves.

4. Hold the Leviathan sigil before your heart. Close your eyes and visualize the great serpent coiling beneath the sea — endless, powerful, watching.

5. Speak the invocation:

"O Leviathan, lord of depths untamed,
Serpent eternal, coil of shadow and flame,
I call thee from abyssal halls,
Where silence reigns and darkness falls.
Embrace me in your endless sea,
Let chaos cleanse and set me free."

6. Dip your fingers into the bowl, then anoint your forehead, chest, and wrists, feeling the cold abyss flow through you.

7. Sit in silence, allowing sensations to rise. Let visions, emotions,

or shadows surface unbidden.

8. When complete, thank Leviathan aloud, snuff the candle, and close your circle.

Banishing Ritual: Parting the Waters

Leviathan's presence is potent and can overwhelm. A careful banishing ritual is essential.

Tools Needed:

White candle

Freshwater and sea salt mixture

Sage or palo santo incense

Mirror for reflection

Procedure:

1. Light the white candle and incense.

2. Sprinkle the saltwater mixture in a sweeping motion around your space, envisioning the darkness receding.

3. Hold the mirror and gaze into it, affirming:

"I release the waters, the shadows, the coil,
The depths return to their sacred soil.
Leviathan's tide ebbs now from me,
In light and peace, so mote it be."

4. Extinguish candle and incense safely, then cleanse yourself by washing hands and face.

Correspondences for Leviathanic Work

Element, Water (Oceans, Seas, Rivers)

Planet, Neptune, sometimes Saturn

Day, Thursday (Jupiter), Wednesday (Mercury)

Color, Deep Blue, Black, Indigo

Incense, Myrrh, Seaweed, Frankincense

Crystal, Obsidian, Jet, Aquamarine

Metal, Tin, sometimes Lead

Animal Symbol, Serpent, SeaSerpent, Leviathan

Direction, West (the direction of the setting sun and water)

Tarot, The Moon, The Hanged Man

Associated Emotions, Envy, Rage, Chaos, Transformation

Psychological Notes on Working with Ritual

Leviathanic ritual is as much an internal journey as an external act. The invocation invites the practitioner to experience submerged psychic material — suppressed rage, envy, grief, creative chaos — emerging from depths long hidden.

Approach the ritual with reverence and caution. Do not rush the process.

Keep a journal to record visions, emotions, and insights.

Practice grounding techniques after each ritual to maintain

balance.

Adaptations for Modern Practitioners

Contemporary occultists may adapt these rituals using digital sigils, recorded chants, or working with personal tokens rather than traditional tools. The key is intentionality and focus on Leviathan's qualities: depth, transformation, and shadow.

Leviathan's ritual legacy is vast and formidable. To summon this ancient force is to open to the dark sea of the self, to dive into chaos and emerge — not unscathed, but reborn.

CHAPTER SIXTEEN: CHANTS AND HIDDEN KNOWLEDGE

Within the shadows of occult lore, Leviathan is not merely summoned through ritual alone — it is called forth through ancient chants, whispered incantations, and guarded secrets that echo through the corridors of hidden knowledge. These sonic and symbolic keys unlock doors to Leviathan's abyssal power, bridging the mortal and the monstrous, the conscious and the submerged.

This chapter unearths these secret voices — the chants and arcane wisdom that have been passed down in hushed tones or encoded in forgotten grimoires. To speak Leviathan's name is to speak in the language of the deep, a tongue woven from chaos, silence, and primal force.

The Nature of Leviathan's Voice: Silence and Sound

Leviathan's voice is paradoxical — it is both the roar of the crashing ocean and the deafening silence beneath the waves. In occult tradition, true communication with Leviathan transcends spoken words; it manifests as a vibration felt deep in the bones, a resonance that stirs the primal self.

The Silence Before the Call: Many practitioners speak of a moment of profound silence — a psychic stillness — that precedes the invocation. It is the abyss waiting to speak, a dark breath held before the flood.

The Chant as Vessel: The chant or incantation is less a demand and more a vessel — a form into which Leviathan's chaotic energy flows. Proper intonation, rhythm, and cadence become crucial, as the chant shapes the psychic currents.

Ancient and Modern Leviathanic Chants

Few chants attributed explicitly to Leviathan survive in classical grimoires, but modern occultists and mystics have reconstructed and composed incantations inspired by its nature and mythos.

Here are examples of chants used to call or attune to Leviathan's power:

The Abyssal Coil Chant

This chant mimics the cyclical, coiling nature of Leviathan's energy, spoken in a slow, deliberate rhythm.

"Serpent coil beneath the sea,
Boundless dark, consume in me,
Endless spiral, deep abyss,
Whisper now your shadowed kiss."

Repeat thrice, allowing the voice to deepen and lengthen with each cycle, imagining the serpent's coils tightening around the heart, awakening buried power.

The Dark Sea Invocation

A chant designed to invoke Leviathan's domain — the endless ocean of chaos and transformation.

> "O mother of drowned realms,
> Dark tide that overwhelms,
> Swallow me in your endless night,
> Transform, consume, ignite."

This is spoken softly at first, then rising to a crescendo, before fading back into silence — mimicking the tide's rise and fall.

Hidden Names and Sacred Words

In esoteric practice, names carry power beyond their letters. Leviathan is sometimes addressed through secret names or variations designed to access specific aspects of its force.

Leviahann: An ancient variant emphasizing the serpent's "voice" or "roar," used in rites of revelation and vision.

Rahab: A name linked with Leviathan in Hebrew texts, associated with chaos and the primordial sea; invoked to harness destructive and transformative power.

Tsaphon: From Near Eastern mythologies, a hidden mountain or abyssal place associated with sea monsters, often linked to Leviathan's domain. Chanting this name calls forth the hidden depths of shadow and power.

Practitioners often combine these names with sigils, glyphs, or elemental sounds such as the hum of water or the crackle of fire to create layered invocations.

The Role of Sound and Vibration in Leviathanic Magick

Sound is not merely symbolic but energetic. The frequency of chants influences the practitioner's nervous system, opening channels to unconscious realms where Leviathan's power resides.

Monotone humming: Sustained, low-frequency humming mimics the endless depths of the sea and can induce trance states conducive to spirit contact.

Tonal modulation: Shifting pitch in chants mirrors the undulating waves and serpent coils, amplifying the transformative effect.

Use of drums or water percussion: Rhythmic pounding or water sounds recreate the ocean's heartbeat, anchoring ritual in elemental reality.

Hidden Knowledge: The Esoteric Teachings of Leviathan

Beyond chants lie the hidden teachings guarded by initiates who understand Leviathan not as a simple entity but as a gateway to profound transformation.

The Flood as Purification: Leviathan represents the floodwaters that wash away false identities, illusions, and stagnation. This destructive chaos is necessary for psychic renewal — a brutal cleansing that leaves nothing untouched.

The Coil as Eternity and Enclosure: The serpent's coil symbolizes not just infinite cycles but the tension between freedom and confinement. To work with Leviathan is to hold this tension consciously — embracing limits while reaching for boundlessness.

Envy and Shadow Integration: Leviathan's association with envy is not a curse but a mirror of desire and shadow. Through facing these emotions honestly, the initiate accesses hidden reservoirs of motivation and power previously locked beneath shame or repression.

The Abyss as Threshold: Leviathan is the threshold guardian to the abyss — that void where ego dissolves and pure being emerges. The initiate must be willing to confront annihilation to be reborn.

Warnings and Protections in Voice Work

Calling Leviathan through chant and invocation is not without peril. The power unleashed is primal and unpredictable.

Always begin and end voice work with grounding and banishing rituals.

Use protective amulets such as black obsidian or jet stones.

Work with trusted guides or within a safe ritual framework.

Monitor emotional and psychic responses carefully — overwhelming feelings may arise.

The Secret Transmission: Oral Tradition and the Passing of Leviathan's Voice

In many occult circles, Leviathanic chants and incantations are passed through oral tradition, whispered in secrecy, often encoded in metaphor and allegory.

This secret transmission protects the potency of the words and ensures only those prepared may hear and wield the serpent's voice.

Leviathan's voice is both a call and a test — a soundless roar beneath the waves, a shadowed whisper stirring the deep. To learn its chant is to learn the language of the abyss — to dance with chaos, to surrender to transformation, and to emerge forever changed.

CHAPTER SEVENTEEN – LEVIATHAN'S SYMBOLIC WEB: CONNECTIONS TO MYTHIC CREATURES AND OCCULT ARCHETYPES

Leviathan does not exist in isolation. Across cultures and esoteric traditions, it entwines with a vast symbolic network—sharing traits, energies, and lessons with other mythic beasts and occult archetypes. To understand Leviathan fully is to map its intricate relationships within this web of darkness and power.

This chapter journeys through these connections, revealing how Leviathan resonates as both a singular force and a node within a greater cosmic tapestry.

Leviathan and the Dragon: The Primordial Serpent of Chaos and Creation

Perhaps the most immediate kin to Leviathan is the Dragon—

the archetypal serpent that appears worldwide as a symbol of primordial chaos, wisdom, and power.

Shared Elemental Nature: Both Leviathan and dragons embody the elemental forces of water and earth, often depicted as serpentine or reptilian creatures commanding vast, chaotic energies beneath the surface of reality. Their connection to the deep earth and ocean depths links them to hidden knowledge and the unconscious.

Chaos and Creation: Dragons and Leviathan are both agents of destruction and genesis. They consume and dissolve to clear the path for new life. The dragon's fiery breath and Leviathan's tidal surge symbolize the complementary forces of fire and water—both vital for transformation.

Mythic Overlaps: In some mythologies, Leviathan merges with dragon-like forms or is seen as a sea dragon or sea serpent. This fluid identity underscores its liminal power and resistance to fixed form.

Leviathan and Jörmungandr: The World Serpent of Norse Myth

Across the northern seas, Leviathan finds a close counterpart in Jörmungandr, the immense World Serpent of Norse legend.

Encircling the World: Like Leviathan's eternal coil, Jörmungandr encircles Midgard (the human world), biting its own tail in a cosmic ouroboros symbolizing cyclic time and the eternal return.

Harbinger of Ragnarok: Jörmungandr is destined to battle the god Thor during Ragnarok, the twilight of the gods. This apocalyptic clash mirrors Leviathan's role as an agent of destruction and renewal, the chaos that both ends and begins worlds.

Depth and Shadow: Both serpents dwell in primordial waters—Leviathan in the abyssal sea, Jörmungandr in the encircling ocean

—representing the dark depths of the unconscious, fate, and the shadow aspects of existence.

Leviathan and Tiamat: The Babylonian Chaos Mother

From Mesopotamian myth emerges Tiamat, a monstrous sea dragon and mother of chaos closely aligned with Leviathan's dark feminine aspect.

Primordial Chaos and Motherhood: Tiamat, like Leviathan, is a symbol of the chaotic sea and the dark womb from which creation and destruction flow. She embodies the wild feminine force—capricious, destructive, and fertile.

Cosmic Battle and Creation: Tiamat's battle with the storm god Marduk parallels Leviathan's mythic struggles, where chaos is subdued but never destroyed—transformed into order's foundation.

Symbol of the Dark Feminine: Occult traditions often link Leviathan's shadow feminine aspect with Tiamat's archetype—both as figures of chaos, transformation, and the shadow mother.

Leviathan and the Abyss: The Occult Archetype of the Void

In occult philosophy, Leviathan often embodies or guards the Abyss—the symbolic void between mundane consciousness and higher spiritual realms.

Guardian of the Threshold: Leviathan stands as the sentinel of the abyssal gulf that separates ego from the divine or cosmic consciousness. Crossing this abyss requires surrender to the unknown, risking annihilation.

Shadow and Transformation: The abyss represents the

psychological and spiritual void where false selves dissolve. Leviathan's presence within this archetype emphasizes the necessity of confronting shadow and chaos for true awakening.

Path of Initiation: Many occult systems place Leviathan as a central figure in the initiatory journey through darkness, embodying the trial by chaos that precedes rebirth.

Leviathan and Lilith: The Dark Feminine in Occult Mythos

Leviathan's dark feminine energy resonates closely with Lilith, the archetype of the rebellious, untamed woman in many occult and mystical traditions.

Shared Themes of Rebellion and Independence: Both embody a refusal to submit—Leviathan as the untamable sea beast, Lilith as the first woman who refused subservience. Their powers lie in wild freedom and shadow sovereignty.

Dark Feminine as Power and Danger: Leviathan and Lilith both carry the duality of life-giving and destructive forces. Their darkness challenges societal norms and invites deep psychic transformation.

Ritual Pairing: Some occult practices invoke Leviathan and Lilith together, recognizing their combined force as the ultimate expression of the shadow feminine — chaos, seduction, rage, and liberation.

Leviathan and the Shadow Archetype: Jungian Reflections

From a psychological perspective, Leviathan is a profound symbol of the Shadow, the hidden, often rejected parts of the self.

Embodiment of Repressed Emotion: Leviathan manifests envy,

rage, grief, and primal chaos—feelings often denied or suppressed. Engaging with Leviathan symbolizes confronting these internal depths.

Integration and Wholeness: Jungian psychology views the Shadow as essential for psychic wholeness. Leviathan's symbolic form helps practitioners embrace their shadow, facilitating growth and transformation.

The Serpent as Psyche's Guide: The serpent form of Leviathan is a classic image of psychic transformation—shedding skin, coiling energy, and rising renewed.

Leviathan and the Elemental Forces: Water and Chaos

Leviathan is fundamentally a force of water, the archetype of emotion, intuition, and the unconscious — but also of chaos, depth, and destruction.

Elemental Magick: In occult elemental systems, Leviathan governs the watery realms — oceans, rivers, rain — connecting practitioners to deep emotional and spiritual currents.

Chaos as Creative Force: Water's fluidity symbolizes change and adaptability, but Leviathan reminds us that beneath calm surfaces lies potential for overwhelming chaos and transformation.

Balancing Elements: Working with Leviathan encourages mastery over not only water but the interplay of elemental forces within the self—fire, earth, air, and water—in a dynamic dance of creation and destruction.

Final Reflections: Leviathan as Nexus of Myth and Magick

Leviathan's vast symbolic network reveals it as a nexus

point where myth, psychology, and occult power converge. Its connections to dragons, serpents, abyssal guardians, and shadow archetypes enrich its role as an entity that both frightens and liberates.

By understanding Leviathan's relationships, the practitioner gains a fuller picture of the dark currents that shape occult practice and inner transformation.

Leviathan is the dark sea in which many myths swim—a living symbol of chaos and order entwined, a beast of shadow and light forever coiling beneath the surface of human consciousness.

CHAPTER EIGHTEEN: SHADOWS IN INK SECRET SCROLLS AND FORBIDDEN TEXTS ON LEVIATHAN

Beyond the widely known grimoires and tomes lies a darker, more forbidden undercurrent of occult writings—ancient scrolls, hidden manuscripts, and cryptic scripts passed hand to hand through secret societies and shadowed cults. These documents whisper of Leviathan not as a mere demon or myth, but as an arcane force so vast and terrible that even the bravest sorcerers feared to name it aloud.

This chapter delves into those hidden texts—fragments of lost knowledge unearthed from the dust of forgotten libraries and coded within esoteric symbols. Their contents reveal Leviathan not only as a cosmic serpent but as a primordial abyssal intelligence, a godlike being whose presence twists reality and fractures the mind.

The Lost Scroll of Khar'Zhul: Leviathan's True Name

Among the most sought-after relics is the Scroll of Khar'Zhul, an ancient parchment discovered deep beneath the ruins of a drowned city in the Mediterranean. Written in a blend of dead languages and arcane sigils, it purportedly contains the "True Name" of Leviathan, a word so potent that its utterance can rend the veil between worlds.

The Nature of the Scroll: The text is fragmented, its edges scorched, but certain passages survive. They speak of Leviathan as the "Coiled Whisper Beyond Time", a presence older than creation, whose breath births storms and whose silence suffocates stars.

The True Name's Power: Inscribed in an untranslatable script, the True Name is said to be a vibrational key unlocking Leviathan's essence. Scholars who attempted to pronounce it report terrifying psychic assaults—visions of drowning, madness, and infinity folding upon itself.

Ritual Usage: The Scroll instructs that the True Name be spoken only within a consecrated circle inscribed with the serpent's coil, during the darkest hour of the new moon, with offerings of saltwater and blood. Its misuse allegedly caused entire cults to vanish without trace.

The Codex Tenebris: Leviathan's Pact and the Abyssal Language

The Codex Tenebris, a medieval manuscript kept under lock in a remote monastery, is believed to contain the language of the abyss—a guttural, shifting tongue through which Leviathan communicates.

A Language Beyond Human Speech: The Codex's text is a complex interweaving of ciphers, unknown glyphs, and musical notation. When chanted in the proper sequence, it is said to summon Leviathan's presence as a vibrational echo, felt in the marrow.

The Pact of the Abyss: The Codex details an ancient pact whereby a sorcerer may bind aspects of Leviathan's power—envy, rage, and the capacity to flood worlds of thought—in exchange for servitude in the shadow realms.

Dark Warnings: Numerous marginal notes, apparently written by terrified monks, warn that breaking the pact condemns the soul to be swallowed by the serpent's endless coils, trapped eternally in psychic drowning.

The Serpent's Manuscript: Forbidden Rituals from the Black Library

Legends tell of the Black Library, a hidden archive beneath the ruins of a shattered cathedral, containing the Serpent's Manuscript—a collection of rituals and invocations so potent they dissolve reality's boundaries.

Rituals of the Coil: The Manuscript describes ceremonies that spiral from whispered chants to frenzied ecstatic states, invoking Leviathan's coiling power to twist time and perception. These rituals often require sacrifices—sometimes symbolic, sometimes disturbingly real.

Psychic Fracturing and Rebirth: Practitioners of the Serpent's Manuscript report entering altered states where self dissolves into an abyssal consciousness—terrifying yet illuminating. It is said to be a path to becoming a "child of the deep," reborn from the crushing depths.

Vanishing of the Initiates: Mysterious disappearances and madness are recurring footnotes in the Manuscript's history. Entire covens vanished after conducting the final ritual known as "The Swallowing Coil."

The Night Whispers: Oral Traditions and Coded Scripts

Not all knowledge of Leviathan exists on parchment. Secret cults and subterranean occult circles pass down Night Whispers—oral transmissions encoded in metaphor and dream language.

The Code of the Deep: Whispers speak of an esoteric cipher—patterns of waves, serpentine tattoos, and rhythmic drumbeats that carry Leviathan's essence between initiates. This hidden language allows communication without words, a silent call beneath reality's surface.

Dream Scripts: Some adepts receive fragments of Leviathan's knowledge in dreams—symbolic scripts formed of flowing water, serpents, and twisting labyrinths. Deciphering these visions is said to reveal personal keys to the abyss.

Guardians of the Whisper: These oral traditions are fiercely protected. Outsiders who attempt to decode the Night Whispers often fall into obsession or madness, swallowed by Leviathan's unfolding coil.

The Manuscript of Drowned Kings: Leviathan as Cosmic Judge

Among the darkest texts is the Manuscript of Drowned Kings, describing Leviathan as the judge of drowned souls and broken kingdoms.

Leviathan as Cosmic Executioner: The manuscript portrays Leviathan not only as a destroyer but as an arbiter of divine retribution, swallowing those who betray cosmic laws beneath the waves.

The Flooded Throne: It speaks of a hidden throne beneath the ocean floor, where Leviathan sits entwined in endless coils, weighing the souls of kings and conquerors before consigning them to oblivion.

Prophecies and Curses: The text contains prophecies warning of a coming age when Leviathan's flood will rise to cleanse the earth, erasing empires and minds alike—an apocalyptic vision both feared and revered by occultists.

Hidden Knowledge as a Double-Edged Sword

The allure of these secret texts is undeniable—a path to power, insight, and transcendence. Yet their knowledge is a double-edged sword, offering illumination wrapped in madness.

Psychic Dangers: Many who seek these hidden scrolls suffer from overwhelming visions, nightmares of drowning and eternal darkness, or fragmented realities where self and abyss merge.

Esoteric Secrecy: The texts are deliberately obscured—written in layered codes, cryptic symbols, and dangerous languages designed to shield the uninitiated.

Ethical Questions: The rituals often demand great sacrifices, both symbolic and literal, challenging the seeker's will, sanity, and soul.

Conclusion: The Endless Coil of Forbidden Knowledge

Leviathan's secret scrolls and hidden texts are more than dusty relics; they are living echoes of the abyss, channels through which ancient, unfathomable forces still whisper and writhe.

To hold these writings is to clutch a fragment of chaos itself—an invitation to dive into darkness deeper than most dare venture. The risk is total consumption by the serpent's coils, yet the prize is a knowledge beyond time, a power submerged beneath all reality.

Leviathan waits in the ink-stained shadows of these forbidden manuscripts—ready to enfold the brave, the foolish, and the damned alike.

CHAPTER NINETEEN: RITUAL WORK WITH LEVIATHAN

To engage Leviathan is to step beyond ordinary ritual practice into the depths of the abyss—a space where order dissolves, primal chaos reigns, and the boundaries between self and other blur into a serpentine coil of shadow and power. This chapter offers meticulously detailed rituals crafted to invoke, work with, and honor Leviathan's fearsome, transformative presence.

These rites demand preparation, reverence, and courage. They are not casual ceremonies but profound initiations into the dark waters where Leviathan dwells.

Preparing the Ritual Space: Creating the Abyss

Leviathan's realm is the primordial sea, endless, dark, and unfathomable. The ritual space must evoke this abyssal atmosphere.

Location: Ideally near a body of water—sea, lake, or river—or a quiet, shadowed room adorned with water symbols.

Circle Casting: Use coarse sea salt, crushed shells, and black obsidian stones to form a circle, symbolizing Leviathan's eternal coil. Trace the serpent's shape within the circle using powdered indigo or dark blue pigment.

Lighting: Use black and deep blue candles, flickering low, to suggest depths and shadows. Place them so their light pools like dim reflections.

Incense: Burn a blend of myrrh, seaweed, and frankincense. The scent evokes oceanic mystery and ancient power.

Offerings: Prepare a bowl of saltwater mixed with drops of wine or pomegranate juice, symbolizing blood and life's fluidity. Offer a small mirror representing the abyssal mirror of the deep.

Ritual One: Invocation of the Coil

This ritual calls Leviathan to coil within the practitioner's spirit, inviting transformation through shadow.

Tools: Leviathan's sigil (drawn or engraved), black candle, bowl of saltwater, serpent-shaped amulet or coil of rope.

Steps:

1. Centering: Sit quietly within the circle, eyes closed, breathing slow and deep. Visualize descending into deep, dark waters—cold, silent, infinite.

2. Lighting the Candle: Light the black candle. Let its flame dance like a flickering abyss.

3. Sigil Activation: Hold the Leviathan sigil before your heart. Breathe onto it thrice, whispering:
"Coil of the deep, serpent of shadow, awaken."

4. Anointing: Dip fingertips into the saltwater offering, touch forehead, chest, and wrists—anointing self as vessel of Leviathan's power.

5. Chanting the Coil: Slowly chant:
"Serpent coil, endless spiral,
Embrace my soul, dark and viral.
From depths unknown, your power bring,
In shadow's clasp, I dance and sing."
Repeat thrice, modulating voice deeper each time.

6. Meditation: Sit in silent communion, feeling the coil tightening within—feel shadow and rage, envy and grief rise, then settle like waves receding.

7. Closing: Thank Leviathan aloud, extinguish the candle, sprinkle remaining saltwater around the circle's edge, releasing the presence gently.

Ritual Two: The Abyssal Pact

For those who seek to bind Leviathan's energies in service or transformation, this rite formalizes the connection.

Tools: The Leviathan sigil, two black candles, bowl of saltwater mixed with pomegranate juice, a silver knife or athame, parchment, and ink.

Steps:

1. Circle Casting: Prepare the space as above.

2. Light Candles: Place one candle on the right, one on the left.

3. Writing the Pact: On parchment, inscribe your name and a vow to honor the powers of Leviathan, calling upon its dark essence to guide and transform.

4. Blood or Ink Anointing: Use the tip of the silver knife to prick the finger lightly, mixing a drop of blood into the ink or saltwater.

5. Pact Recitation: Holding the parchment, recite:
"Leviathan, great coil beneath the sea,
I bind myself to your infinity.
With blood and salt, I seal this vow,
To walk your depths and take your power now."

6. Dipping the Parchment: Submerge the parchment briefly into the saltwater offering.

7. Candle Unity: Light one candle's flame with the other, symbolizing the union of mortal will and abyssal force.

8. Seal the Pact: Fold the parchment and keep it sacred—near your altar or worn on your person.

9. Closing: Extinguish candles one at a time, expressing gratitude.

Ritual Three: The Swallowing Coil — A Journey into the Abyss

This advanced ritual is a psychic journey designed to dissolve ego boundaries and initiate profound transformation.

Tools: Black velvet cloth, black candle, bowl of saltwater, serpent amulet, bell or chime.

Steps:

1. Preparation: Rest in a dark, quiet place. Lay the black velvet cloth on the floor.

2. Casting Circle: Use salt and pigment to draw a large serpent coil

on the cloth.

3. Lighting: Place the candle in the center.

4. Entering the Coil: Sit or lie within the coil. Light the candle.

5. Chanting and Breathwork: Slowly chant the Abyssal Coil Chant (see Chapter Sixteen) while breathing deeply, visualizing the serpent coiling tighter and tighter around your being.

6. Ring the Bell: After the third chant, ring the bell or chime to signify crossing the threshold.

7. Silent Descent: Close eyes and surrender to the darkness, feeling yourself swallowed by Leviathan's endless coils—ego dissolving into dark waters.

8. Vision and Reception: Stay in this liminal state as long as possible, allowing visions, sensations, or insights to arise. Journal afterwards.

9. Grounding: When ready, ring the bell again, visualize rising from the depths, and blow out the candle.

Aftercare: Grounding and Protection

Working with Leviathan's potent energies requires careful aftercare.

Physical Grounding: Eat nourishing food, drink fresh water, and walk barefoot on earth or stone.

Energetic Cleansing: Use sage, palo santo, or salt baths to clear residual energies.

Psychic Protection: Visualize a protective shell or carry obsidian or jet stones.

Reflection: Keep a journal of experiences, emotions, and visions for integration.

Final Words on Ritual Power

Leviathan is not a force to be summoned lightly. Its rituals peel back the layers of reality and psyche, revealing truths that can overwhelm and transform. Respect, preparation, and intent are the keys to safe passage into its dark waters.

When you stand within Leviathan's circle, you are no longer merely human—you are a being poised between chaos and creation, drowning and rebirth, shadow and light.

CHAPTER TWENTY: FINAL WORDS THE SERPENT BENEATH ALL THINGS

At the end of all grimoires, after the invocations have faded into silence and the sigils lie dormant in candle wax and shadow, there comes a moment of stillness—a breathless pause where the practitioner is left alone in the dark, staring into the void they willingly opened. This chapter is that silence. These are the final words, not of ending, but of immersion.

Because with Leviathan, there is no end.

There is only depth.

And the deeper one goes, the more one finds not horror, not salvation, but truth. Raw. Coiled. Infinite.

The Journey Recap: Through Coil, Chaos, and Consciousness

From the first utterance of Leviathan's name, this book has descended through shadowed corridors of esoteric knowledge, myth, ritual, and personal gnosis. We began with Leviathan's ancient presence in forgotten scriptures and half-buried mythologies. But this was never about dusty lore.

This has always been about awakening.

Awakening the coiled serpent beneath your skin.

Awakening the primal sea that churns behind your eyes.

Awakening the envy, the hunger, the rage that has no name—but wears the mask of Leviathan.

Through ritual, chant, invocation, and silence, we have summoned that mask, not to worship, but to see through it—to see what lies beneath the roles we play, beneath our boundaries and limitations.

And what we found was darkness, yes—but not emptiness.

Darkness is not void. It is womb. It is mirror. It is origin.

The Abyss Within: Leviathan as Mirror and Gateway

Every coil of Leviathan is a spiral into the unconscious. Every invocation is an invitation to drown in what you pretend not to feel—shame, desire, fury, grief. But in drowning, there is transformation.

Leviathan does not "possess" in the way lesser spirits do. It devours, not to destroy but to redefine. Those who work with Leviathan rarely return the same. They do not emerge lighter, cleaner, or more virtuous.

They emerge deeper.

Stripped of pretense. Stripped of surface. Still and terrible in their sovereignty.

Because Leviathan teaches what few are willing to learn:

That chaos is not the enemy.
That envy is the root of desire.

That to fall is not to fail—
But to finally touch the bottom,
And from there, see everything.

The Warning Repeated: Not for All

If you've come this far, it means you have tasted something beyond the veil. But be warned once more:

Leviathan is not a path of safety.
This is not love-and-light spirituality.
This is not healing through comfort.
This is healing through cracking open the ego like a drowned shell.

To embrace Leviathan is to embrace pain as teacher, chaos as mentor, and darkness as guide.

It is not for all.

And it should never be offered freely. Those who hear the call will know it. Those who fake it will be undone by it.

Legacy of the Coil: What Remains

Leviathan has no temples, no dogma, no priests.

Its temple is the ocean of your unconscious.
Its altar is the space where your shadow and desire collide.
Its prayer is a silent scream underwater.

And its legacy?

You.

If you have walked this far, you are now part of a lineage of abyss-walkers, serpent-speakers, and coil-bearers. You carry the gnosis that cannot be explained, only embodied.

You know the truth:
That the abyss is not empty.
It waits.
It watches.
It remembers.
And it returns.

The Final Breath

So let this book close as it began—with a whisper, not a roar.

A final breath taken beneath dark waters,
A final gaze into the mirror that does not reflect,
A final word that is not a word at all, but a coil tightening quietly around the soul.

Let Leviathan wrap around you.
Let silence reign.
Let the abyss open.
And when you return—if you return—
Know that you were never alone in the dark.

You were watched.
Held.
Transformed.

You were claimed.

So let the candle die. Let the ink dry. Let the serpent sleep.

But know this:

Leviathan waits. And the deep is never far.

ABOUT THE AUTHOR

Seth Helix is a reclusive practitioner of the arcane arts, known for his unwavering descent into the depths of esoteric darkness. A scholar of forbidden texts and ancient serpentine mythos, Helix has spent decades piecing together the scattered remnants of occult tradition, uncovering truths deliberately buried beneath centuries of silence and fear.

His work is not for the faint of heart. It is born from nights soaked in shadow, from whispered names and coiling dreams that refuse to fade at dawn. Seth does not write to entertain. He writes to awaken, to unsettle, to invite the reader into communion with the forces most choose to deny.

Made in United States
North Haven, CT
19 July 2025